REDISCOVERING THE WISDOM OF

HUMAN NATURE

By

Chet Shupe

Spiritual Freedom Press™

SpiritualFreedomPress.com

Redicovering the Wisdom of Human Nature

How Civilization Destroys Happiness

Chet Shupe

ISBN (Print Edition): 978-1-09830-399-0

ISBN (eBook Edition): 978-1-09830-400-3

CONTENTS

Happiness

We all seek it, but how happy *are* we?

I am happiest on a motorcycle.

I ride the open road with my friends. My bike makes a ski slope out of the whole world.

But I can't ride 24/7.

What percentage of each day are you happy?

Thoreau once said, "The mass of men lead lives of quiet desperation." That quote is famous, because it rings so true.

Wild animals, once captured, are never the same, again.

Animals born in cages are more like humans—often bored, anxious, or depressed.

I think we need to give more thought to what it was like to be human, before civilization caged us.

—Chet Shupe

In Appreciation

Marianne Ferrari, who served as my editor, had a sense that I was onto something when no one else seemed to have a clue. Without her friendship, her support, her concern that we get it right, and her grasp of the reader's perspective, this book wouldn't be nearly what it is. Many passages come directly from her pen.

The book has been written to provide a perspective on mankind's existence that will inspire people to change their way of life. But, ideas are of little value if they are not communicated. If this book brings change, Marianne's contribution to that end will have been every bit as significant as mine.

Introduction

For the purposes of this book, there are only two chapters in the story of mankind. The first chapter unfolded like everything else in the natural world that defined the nature of the evolving human species. That was the environment in which homo sapiens appeared, took hold, then flourished—*at-one with Nature.* These ancestral pre-humans and humans survived on the land in small groups intimately connected by the already ingrained human need for the feelings of safety and belonging provided by the presence of others.

One of the more potent of evolution's special gifts to humanity— our gift of language—made possible the second chapter in the life of our species. Before language, both humans and animals had always lived in the moment, focused on what *is.* Once humans had language, they eventually developed an unnatural relationship with the future. Previously, people had concerned themselves only with the immediate future. After language, we became concerned about the long-term future, even eternity.

Once people were able to talk about the future, they quite naturally began to worry about it. They became afraid of it—afraid of what would happen, afraid they wouldn't be safe in a future yet unknown. Inevitably, they began to use language to create ways to guarantee safety in the future. They learned to make plans, then to organize and carry them out. Thinking they had control of their fate, they began living for the future, instead of in the moment. Ever since then mankind has focused on what *should be*, not on what *is*.

These ancient people had no way of knowing they were unwittingly making a world-changing error, by flirting with the concept of the future. Nor did they realize that every generation after them would suffer, because of it. It felt so natural, at the time, that there was nothing to stop them, or the generations that followed, from carrying that line of thinking to the nth degree…

The result is the modern world in which we live, a world quite separated from the natural world that once cradled humanity. We now live in a world of technology, comforts, and excess, in which we see our possibilities as limited only by our imaginations. We even envision ourselves one-day inhabiting the far reaches of the universe.

In the course of this drastic change, our "chapter two" has become the story of how we lost our connection to our human nature—the emotional and spiritual core that makes us human. We now live in an artificial world of physical and material comforts that wealth provides. Born into this Teflon world, virtually none of us realize that, before chapter two, human life was replete with *spiritual* wealth—the inherent comfort that is missing in our world, today. It is the comfort that comes from the love people experience when depending on each other for survival. Just as friction makes fire, interdependence breeds the deeply threaded love of sisterhoods and brotherhoods—the spiritual wealth that satisfies the hunger of our souls.

For thousands of years, modern humans have lived without this key human comfort, whose absence is making our lives increasingly strained. Nearly all of us are aware—some chronically—of our personal anxieties about the future, guilt about the conduct of our lives, resentment over any number of lacks, injustices, real or imagined slights, boredom, hopelessness, intermittent depression… All of it. At the bottom of that pile of modern woes lies the emotional isolation that causes it all, the lack of love, lack of real intimacy with others, the lack of freedom to express how we really feel, the necessity of repressing our real desires. All of this we tolerate in our modern world, which demands compliance, rather than valuing us as the beings that we are.

Modern life is not fit for humans. Modern life, in fact, is a desert for the soul. For thousands of years, humankind has been stranded in this desert, yet, the "mothballed" soul of every human has remained intact. That is the reason I believe there is a way for us, once again, to feel and behave as the natural humans we are.

This book has been written to break that impasse, and end human blindness to the suffering that institutional life inflicts upon us all. Understanding that the way out of the desert is a way to *be*, not a set of goals or plans, is all it takes to start the process. Once we understand, we can hear the soul's message, again—a message that, once heard, cannot be stilled.

Beneath the umbrella of that understanding, people will gravitate together, drawn by an irrepressible hankering for the intimate, interdependent lives all humans once took for granted. That's how we'll find the people with whom to make real homes, again. Though our lifetimes aren't long enough for us to see humankind's complete return to the natural human way of life, rest assured the process will not cease, once started. Too many people will understand, by then, that *no human can enjoy spiritual wealth, nor can any species long survive, if its members are spiritually imprisoned by force of man-made laws that deny them access to their innate emotional intelligence.* Darwin discovered that we descended from social primates, but that has traditionally been interpreted as applying only to our physical nature. I am saying that it applies to our emotional nature, as well. Indeed, only by being true to our emotional nature can we find contentment.

The Coronavirus pandemic came upon us after this book had gone to press, but I was able to add the following Coda: "The Coronavirus Crisis—A Lesson on Spiritual Connection" discusses how our reactions to crises, particularly this one, shed spiritual light on the nature of our circumstances.

"Comparing Realities," is a table near the end of the book, which brings the entire thesis of this book into sharp focus with clear, concise language. Each row covers a different category of human needs and shows how they fare in natural human life vs. modern institutional life. The glossary, also near the end, clarifies my usage of terms. A brief, but comprehensive statement of what this book is about can be found at the end, in a PowerPoint presentation entitled *How Would Human Life Organize Itself, if People were Free to be True to How they Feel?*

CHAPTER ONE

There is a Message in Emotional Pain

How Civilization Destroys Happiness

Just by doing what they feel like doing, individual humans, elephants, and fireflies, alike, unknowingly serve and perpetuate the life of their species. Like them, no lion, or whale, or worm in the ground ever knows that the volition preceding its every action was organically programmed over eons, through trial-and-error, by evolution.

Today, no king on a throne, no modern serf toiling in a cubicle, no druggie shooting up in an alley realizes that the powerful needs and desires that drive him are, in fact, a damaged form of that same primordial heritage—the *civilized remnants* of evolution's organic programming. Yet that programming—in the original form, which still exists in Nature—*is* the map of life on earth. In the natural world—the real world where mastodons, dinosaurs, then, homo sapiens once thrived—that powerful programming spurred every living being to love doing the things that best helped its species to flourish.

So powerful, so embedded in the architecture of natural life is this emotional programming of living beings that I call it the Law of Life:

To serve life, do things that feel good, and avoid doing things that result in emotional pain.

Doing what feels good, not what hurts, is the one thing that makes sense to every living being. So, the "Law of Life" works flawlessly—*in the natural world.* This doesn't mean suffering is nonexistent in Nature. Rather, it underscores the fact that, in Nature, individuals unfailingly react to every circumstance in a way that maximizes pleasure. According to the Law of Life, the behaviors of individuals in Nature will always be the ones that minimize pain, thus optimize the likelihood that their species will flourish.

The Law of Life applies to civilized humans, as much as it once did to pre-humans and the earliest humans. But we modern humans left the natural world and built our own institutional one—an error that has placed us on the "wrong side" of the Law of Life. We serve another master. Indeed, as subjects of legal systems, we regularly defy the Law of Life, for the sake of our own survival, within the modern paradigm. Consequently, we suffer in numerous ways. In order to make a living, workers go to jobs they hate. Wives remain in meaningless, even abusive relationships, out of fear they couldn't support themselves and their children. People endure endless lines of traffic, to get to work.

When we experience pain, as in the examples above, it's because our souls are sending us an alert message—a serious warning that is always the same: *"You are not serving life!"* This suffering is not due to any fault of our own. We didn't choose to disobey the Law of Life. We disobey it, because we were born into civilized cultures, where we're not free to honor it.

Even the people who invented civil rule weren't at fault. Their collective error was inevitable, given that evolution had gifted us with languaged minds. Our unique linguistic skills enabled humans to do something that no previous being on earth could do—to create our own social order and put aside the natural social order that evolution built into us.

When humans imposed moral edicts, believing they could make life better, the suffering that resulted from breaking the Law of Life began immediately. But, because people didn't know about Nature's law, they interpreted the suffering as being caused by mankind's sinful nature. Their evidence for this was the fact that people seemed incapable of faithfully following all the rules. *No one measured up.* People seemed possessed with the desire to misbehave. What in-fact possesses us is our inborn desire to obey the Law of Life. But, as a result of our belief in civil law, we see ourselves as sinners, when we "slip," by answering that inner voice—never realizing that such "sins" are natural acts inspired by our inborn desire to take care of life.

Since the moment humans began judging themselves as sinful, for transgressing in this way, everything humanity has organized and controlled has worked against our happiness and against the ultimate survival of our species. If we are ever again to experience the contentment of sisterhood and brotherhood that our kind once took for granted, and if our species is to survive this six-thousand-year-old episode of self-imposed punishment, the time must come when we stop chastising people for obeying the Law of Life, and start honoring each other when we behave like normal humans.

The emotional suffering our predecessors so innocently caused is painful, but our languaged minds have found a remarkably direct way to survive it. They manage the pain simply by doubling down on their belief in civilization. They believe civil rule can deliver the future it promises, and they keep believing it without evidence, historical or otherwise, to support it.

Over thousands of years of human life, history has chronicled the rise and fall of many civilizations. It's a well-recognized, thus predictable pattern. Yet, when a system of civil rule fails, we humans take no message from the chaos inherent to these failures, or from the human suffering that heralds them. The message of the suffering is lost on humanity. It carries no weight, relative to our tenacious belief that we will "get it right" the next time.

So, we continue to ignore the consequences of not honoring the Law of Life, taking immense comfort in the idealized future we *think* lies in wait—once we get it right. My concern is that the suffering and associated chaos of civil failures will continue until no humans are left to suffer. What's needed is an intervention, which will occur when humans discover the Law of Life, and figure out how to comply with it by re-establishing sisterhoods and brotherhoods.

I am sure that humans never would have imposed moral laws, had they realized that outlawing natural human behavior would sentence mankind to thousands of years of pointless suffering. But, once civil rule existed, the damage was done. Because of the brain's remarkable ability to adapt, we immediately became dependent on institutions, states, and governments for a sense of purpose, meaning, identity, and survival, itself. Once dependent, our minds had no choice but to take on many other beliefs, to help us manage the suffering that our dependence on civil rule imposed. We found emotional solace through a panoply of beliefs, each promising a better future—belief in religion, ideology, money, science, education, or progress, etc.

When obeying rules, rather than the feelings of our souls, we are not taking care of life. As a consequence, our circumstances eventually become so miserable that beliefs and their promised futures can no longer quell the suffering. That's the point at which people start turning to drugs for relief, and sometimes even suicide, which results when the pain of not being free to take care of life overpowers the will to live. That's how bad things can get in a civil culture, while our languaged minds—still believing in the power of reason to solve our problems—continue on, blissfully unaware of the significance of the suffering. Through this suffering, our souls are trying to tell us something—that, in our effort to control the future through the force of law, we are not solving anything. Indeed, we are making things worse.

One of the many ways the civilized mind unknowingly discounts the suffering caused by institutional subjugation, is to mistake symptoms for problems. No program or plan can end domestic violence or suicide. Both conditions are reactions to, and symptoms of, the emotional suffering that blights human life, under civil rule.

It's essential to distinguish between symptoms and problems. Suicide and domestic violence are not the problem. Both are symptoms. For every suicide, and for every woman who dies at the hand of her spouse, there are hundreds who go on living in intense emotional distress. *Suffering is the problem*. But it's also a symptom of the *real underlying problem*: Modern humans are not free to honor the Law of Life. When our languaged minds finally recognize the real problem, and allow us the freedom to honor the Law of Life, domestic violence, suicide, and countless other symptoms of institutional bondage will cease.

Fact: Our souls are being severely abused under civil rule. That is the message modern people need to receive. Yet, the opposite occurs. We go around behaving as if our actions were not futile—as if our lives were not burdened with loneliness, boredom, dysfunctional family relationships, repressed romantic feelings, and anxiety. We behave as if the suffering didn't exist. We have become experts at hiding our suffering, at times even from ourselves.

If people had any idea that we are living in denial of the Law of Life, and how powerfully doing so offends our souls, they would be shocked to the core of their being, just as I was years ago when it occurred to me. From our soul's perspective, living in denial of the Law of Life is akin to solitary confinement. In effect, we're like animals raised in cages—suffering, but never knowing how badly, because the cage is all we've ever known. One thing is certain. An animal in a cage can't do the things it would do—the things it naturally loves doing—if it were free to survive normally. It can never get high on life, no matter how nice the cage.

As civilized beings, we, too, are emotionally caged, and can't get high on life. The only advantage we have, over a caged animal, is that we *can* get high on the promise of beliefs—and that's why we hold beliefs so sacred. Beliefs, indeed, are all we have with which to placate our souls, because we are not free to do so naturally, by taking care of life.

All animate beings have evolved with an innate addiction to the satisfaction that comes from taking care of life. Under civil rule, we modern humans have become addicted, instead, to *the anticipation of future satisfaction promised by beliefs*. Not free to honor the law of life by living in the moment, it's the only emotional comfort a civil culture can provide. We need to recover from our addiction to beliefs. Until we do, we'll never recognize our need for one another. Recognizing that need is essential, if humans are ever again to get high on life.

We all know that recovering from an addiction is not easy. The person must first admit to being addicted. Then, the pain associated with the addiction must become so severe that the affected individual wants to do something about it. The same is true of recovering from our addiction to beliefs. Despite the difficulty, recovery from belief addiction *is* happening in our world. Mankind's suffering is now so great that people find themselves increasingly incapable of getting relief through beliefs. This is most evident in religion: The number of people who no longer believe in God has increased dramatically, in recent years.

Though many no longer find comfort in religious beliefs, we still find comfort in secular ones—belief in the future promised by money, institutions, law, marriage, science, and progress. So long as we remain addicted to beliefs, our souls will continue to burden us with increasing pain. It's evolution's way of punishing us for not taking care of life. Eventually, the day will come when the pain is so great that our beliefs can no longer hold it at bay. On that day, we will no longer be able to believe in anything that promises a better future. We will stand face-to-face with the reality of the moment, for the first time in our lives.

As scary as that thought seems, now, I think we will discover something remarkable, once we recover from the shock of it all:

Human beings are not afraid of reality—not with our sisters and brothers by our side.

We were born to celebrate reality the same way animals do, the same way humans always did, before institutions existed. That spiritually free humans are capable of living happy, contented, decent, and self-respecting lives is evident in the lifestyle of the Pirahã people, who still live a prehistoric way of life, in their ancestral villages, deep in the Amazon. (Chapter 8) When our beliefs have all finally evaporated, so will the idealized futures we now strive for. We will quite naturally turn to the people around us for the material and emotional support inherent to sisterhoods and brotherhoods. Those relationships will enable us to live in the moment, a joy that has been lost to mankind for thousands of years. In the reality of the moment, we will rejoin the other lifeforms on this planet in life's eternal celebration—not by free will, but as the inevitable result of having recognized reality.

CHAPTER TWO

Spiritual Obligations vs. Legal ones

You can take human beings out of Nature,

but you can't take Nature out of human beings.

When human beings belonged to the natural world, we lived like the animals, on the land, and far more exposed than now to the dangers one encounters in Nature. Each species—including humans—lived, not by plans, but in the present moment. All individual choices and actions were directed by instincts honed and handed down through millennia. Every individual's instincts represented the sum-total of that species' instinctual—its evolutionary—wisdom, to date.

Instincts don't impose rules of behavior. They work in a far more elemental way, by causing individuals to "feel like" doing what best serves the life of the species, given the situation at hand. This body of evolutionary information is so voluminous that it supplies the necessary answer to every situation that any human or animal may encounter in the natural world. Schemes and plans, such as those we humans depend upon, today, play no role in the natural way of life.

For each individual's response to every situation, feelings sparked by instincts were the drivers behind the action taken. That's because feelings represent the sum-total of evolutionary wisdom gained from all the successes and failures of countless individuals over eons of time. The overarching result of the intimate connection animate beings have with feelings is the amazing order we see in the natural world. Natural life works, because of this organic order whose origins trace back to the first stirrings of life, on earth. This order has made it possible for countless lifeforms to coexist and thrive in sufficient harmony for life on this planet to flourish.

Life is much different for civilized humans. Civilized lives are not ordered by Nature, but by each individual's compliance with rules instituted by artificial systems of order. The only time we modern people are even remotely free to do what we feel like doing is when we are on vacation. Hence, two worlds exist: We now live in the world of human civilization, where we can do what we feel like doing only when on vacation. We once lived in the natural world, where, in essence, animals are on vacation all the time, because they always do what they feel like doing. That doesn't mean wild animals are unruly, because as we have seen—Nature has order, an order that humans, too, participated in, long ago. The difference between animals and modern humans is that animals march to a different drummer. They do what they feel like doing, never knowing that their innate wisdom is governing their every behavior.

The loss of our freedom was our own doing. We humans stepped outside the natural paradigm—the natural order—when we became civilized, a few thousand years ago. Ever since, we've been governed by institutions and the laws they impose, to create order in civil cultures. Our survival is now so dependent on complying with legal obligations that we've lost virtually all sense of what we might do, and what our relationships would be like, if we were free to be true to our feelings.

Inside the modern civilized paradigm, we have to work to make a living, by doing things in which we have no emotional investment. We *are* emotionally invested in money, because we need it to survive, but not in the things we have to do to make it. If we ever let go of our emotional investment in money, and the institutions that organize our lives around it, our natural emotions will suddenly be free to come to the fore, again. Remove the artificial rules, and the natural paradigm reasserts itself. Our feelings will again infuse us with that innate affinity for specific behaviors that are intrinsic to the natural order for homo sapiens.

This is possible for all of us, right now, because, underneath our civilized exterior, we humans have the same emotional make-up as pre-civilized people did. We are what we have always been—animals. Like all animals, we possess the innate emotional intelligence to be orderly. But, unlike other animals, we abandoned our emotional investment in the natural order, hence, we are not living according to our natural human way of life. All the other animals kept their investment in natural order. If they *had* allowed themselves to be trapped into artificial lives, as we have, the order we find so amazing, in the natural world, would not exist, today.

As it stands, now, our very survival is so dependent on our obedience to legal obligations that it's hard for us to believe that humans were once born into the life of a natural world ordered by the "spiritual obligations" that arise from the soul, which, in all animate beings, is the repository of evolutionary wisdom. In the natural world, every individual is born with the desire to contribute to order.

Homo Sapiens is a social species—social, because no individual human can physically survive the natural world, alone. Our instinct for close interconnectedness is akin to what researchers have documented among chimpanzees and baboons. In the era during which our species evolved and thrived on earth, we survived as our social primate cousins did—by bonding together in extended family groups of, probably, 30 to 40 individuals.

Over millions of years of living that way, we humans evolved into emotional and spiritual beings with a deep-set need for the sense of wellbeing that can only come from close, trusting, interdependence. Intimacy and spiritual freedom were not mutually exclusive in the closely bonded families that existed, then, because the social fabric amongst those people was based on give-and-take, and on an absence of pretense that made the frank expression of any feeling—even of anger—the norm.

What a far cry from life, today. Such close, yet spiritually free relationships bound us together, as one, in mutual reliance and shared spiritual obligation. In families of this kind, Homo Sapiens thrived, and developed into a species capable of empathy and love, yet, equally capable of killing to protect, or even of sacrificing their own individual lives, to save their brethren.

Remarkably, these unbreakable bonds combined freedom *and* belonging. Each action taken was preceded by a desire that rose from within. Each desire was heartfelt, because it came from one's own soul. Among these people, no danger or uncertainty could still the spirit of a human being. Only loneliness could.

Among both animals and humans, our spiritual obligations to each other spring from powerful desires—in some cases desires more powerful than an individual's will to live. An example of this is seen when desperate hunger drives lions to put themselves in jeopardy, by threatening a troop of baboons. The male baboons fulfill their spiritual obligations by rushing to confront the lions, despite the chance that some might lose their lives.

The lives of those baboons have meaning, in large part, *because of their spiritual obligations*, which are so powerful that, to fulfill them, they are instinctively willing to place their lives at risk, to protect the group of individuals they love. This instinct exists in other social primate males, particularly homo sapiens. *If we men don't have something in our lives that's worth dying for, then we have nothing to live for. It's as simple as that.*

The natural human way of life I have described was rejected, when civilization replaced it, several thousand years ago. That was the trigger that caused humans to emotionally disconnect from one another, and from life's meaning. The way of life we live, nowadays, bears little resemblance to the natural human way of life which once was the incubator, then, the spiritual home that nurtured our species. Uncountable anxieties and contradictions have now replaced the self-evident sense of security and spiritual freedom that our ancestors took for granted. Yet, only milliseconds of evolutionary time have passed, thus our bodies and, most importantly, our emotions, remain unchanged, despite the dramatic changes in the way we live.

Our world is completely different, now—almost entirely man-made, and separated from Nature and the elements. We are surrounded by technology, artificial substances and objects, and subjected to anxieties and other emotional stresses that would be incomprehensible to our ancestors. Nevertheless, we retain *all* our instincts, despite the fact that our survival requires us to repress most of them. We even perceive the natural world as foreign, because *our* relationships are defined, not by how we feel, but by the legal obligations that define order in our civilized world. We're so steeped in legal obligations that we don't even recognize spiritual obligations exist, much less that they-alone maintain the order that we find in Nature—the order that our souls would embrace, if only we were spiritually free.

Our emotional lives are so repressed that, as civilized beings, we entirely overlook the significance of our feelings. Feelings have no place in our way of life, which is dictated by our belief that life is a rational process. To us, feelings are not the source of *order*. They are, instead, the source of *dis*order, because feelings are the culprit whenever we fail to follow the rules! Thus, we learn, early on, that feelings must not be allowed to influence our decisions, at all. We think all decisions should be based exclusively on evidence and logic. What a cold, meaningless, detached world.

Is civilization right? Can human behavior really be explained rationally? *No, of course not.* If reason were, in fact, based exclusively on logic and evidence, then, deciding to have sex would have nothing to do with *desire*. Deciding to eat would have nothing to do with *hunger*. Deciding to enjoy a sunset would have nothing to do with *beauty*. Donning a jacket would have nothing to do with the discomfort of the evening *chill*. And a mother's excitement in preparing for all the children to come home for Christmas would have nothing to do with *love*.

Each of those scenarios demonstrates the deep significance of emotions in human behavior. I think we moderns have it dead wrong. I say: Emotions—not reason—drive life.

Physiologically, it's pretty simple. The brain activity required to produce feelings is enormous, compared to that of rational thought. Rational thought is nothing more than a series of what-if questions— what if I do this, what if I do that, what if I do the other? After evaluating the likely result of each imagined activity, we then choose the behavior we think will best fulfill our desire.

Rational thought is utterly simple, compared to what goes on in our subconscious minds. Rational thinking is the only brain activity that occurs consciously, in any living being. That's why we're aware of it. By nature, we are unaware of the incredibly complex subconscious brain activity that produces each and every feeling we experience, such as love or hunger, anger or empathy, joy or fear, etc.

The fact that we are only aware of brain activity that produces conscious choices makes it both natural and unsurprising that we believe we have free will. But, by believing that, we are overlooking something of unimaginable significance—that our behaviors are not driven by free will. They are driven by the desire to satisfy feelings produced by the subconscious mind. Producing feelings is the subconscious mind's most important function.

The subconscious mind—human or animal—is the sole source of order in the natural world. It produces feelings which inspire, in each individual, the behaviors required for the species to flourish. Despite all the knowledge we have acquired, we civilized humans remain blind to the significance of feelings, and the subconscious mind that produces them.

Think of it this way. To decide is to prefer one thing over others, and preference is the essence of bias. In the case of biological intelligence, the subconscious mind produces the emotional biases required to make choices. We clearly make conscious choices. But, through the relative strength of our various feelings, our subconscious minds exercise absolute control over every choice we make.

We moderns stay fixated, instead, on reason and logic, as the source of human decisions and actions. Unaware of the significance of feelings, when we decide, for example, to eat something, or to love someone, we think we have made a rational choice. We decide to eat, and to love, paying no attention to the fact that neither choice would be available to us, if we had no feelings to satisfy. *Without feelings, we would have no will—free or otherwise. There would be nothing to animate us, thus, no evidence of life, at all.*

Feelings are the messages through which our subconscious mind informs our conscious mind of what it needs to know. Hunger tells the conscious mind, "It's time to eat." Feelings of love tell the conscious mind, "I really need this person in my life." Of course, we can act as though we have free will, by pretending we are hungry, when we're not, or pretending that we love someone we do not love. But, to act in ways that betray how we feel is to be spiritually dishonest—which is a betrayal of ourselves, of the other person, and—most ominously—of life, itself. It's unlikely we'll ever have reason to pretend hunger. But, as subjects of legal obligations, we have manifest reasons to pretend love—a spiritual dishonesty that results in a lot of human suffering.

Our blindness to the significance of feelings confers on us something akin to the dementia we see in the elderly. Unaware that feelings control our decisions, the conscious mind always thinks it is right, and in control. Hence, people with clinical dementia have no way to realize they are behaving strangely, when their subconscious minds produce such feelings as anger, which inspire them to do things inappropriate to their circumstances. Without realizing it, people with dementia are being taken on a bad ride by subconscious processes over which they have no control.

In a similar way, all of civilized humanity is being taken on its own version of a bad ride. For civilized people, the problem isn't dementia, but the unverifiable beliefs our subconscious minds must accept as true, in order to materially and emotionally survive the impositions of civil rule. The contradictions so rife in our present world—such as one person's unverifiable belief that capitalism will save us, vs. another's unsubstantiated belief that only communism or a specific religion will—are evidence of the wrong turn humanity took when our predecessors started controlling human behavior artificially, by force of law. To survive the emotional insult of that mistake, people have been ignoring the significance of their feelings for thousands of years. Thus, civilized people see, as normal, the suffering they endure at the hands of legal subjugation. Modern humans suffer the effects of broken homes, spousal violence, loneliness, and all humanity suffers a background anxiety tinged with the guilt we feel as witnesses to habitat destruction—all the while, seeing it as normal.

But this suffering is not normal. Through it all, our souls have been screaming to us that we *are* off course, but we're not listening— so convinced are we that our conscious minds, via the power of pure reason, will solve all problems, given time. Most painfully, we ignore the source of our suffering—humanity's original mistake, which took us away from the life evolution had given us.

What was the nature of that earlier life? In that natural way of life, people lived in the unfolding moment. Life usually worked out, because our way of life was governed by Nature, through our feelings. The sizes of our families were stable, for example, and we never worried about the future, because we had no way to control it. Bonded, as we were, in interdependent relationships, we felt confident that we could deal with any uncertainty the future might throw at us. And, because we needed one another to feel secure, we loved the members of our social groups unconditionally, just as all other social primates still do.

Life seemed simple. There were no "shoulds." People did what they *felt like doing.* Evolutionary wisdom is so well versed in the ways of the natural world that it provided the answers for all possible situations. It was this instinctual preparation for the uncertainties of life that made human survival possible in the natural world. Our innate wisdom anticipated all possible outcomes so well that people avoided most problems, before they occurred, and bonded in ways that prepared them to effectively manage the ones that couldn't be avoided. An example of this is the instinct of homo sapiens to bond in social groups—a way of life which evolved, because no human can face a lion, alone.

We don't have to face lions, in the modern world, but the pain of loneliness is now endemic. We are lonely, in effect, because we are not socially bonded—and not socially bonded, as a result of not having to face lions. Truth be told, it is only because the natural world is dangerous that our instinct to love one another evolved. If we could recognize this fact, we modern humans would much better understand our own human nature. It is an understanding that would change everything.

You can take human beings out of Nature, but you can't take Nature out of human beings. We were created to live in the natural world where all sorts of dangers exist that we could never manage alone. Even today, our emotional make-up is the same one evolution gave us to cope with the exigencies of the natural world. The natural world is the only place where we emotionally fit. Yet, here we are in the modern world, where there is no place to satisfy our innate feelings. Indeed, we don't even have stable homes. As long as we remain in this modern world, loneliness may well be the most omnipresent of our problems. But, in truth, it is just the tip of the iceberg of our suffering.

A way of life in which people naturally love one another, and in which relationships work, without special effort—or intent, or even thought—seems like a nice way to live. What could possibly have caused our subconscious minds to produce feelings that inspired mankind to leave all that behind?

CHAPTER THREE

Language: A Curse *AND* A Blessing

What did cause our ancestors to discard our natural way of life so casually that they were unaware of having discarded anything of significance. It's all because of language. As our linguistic skills evolved, there came a time when humans could talk about what might happen decades in the future. Other species have language, too, but their vocalizations do not enable them to share concerns about the distant future. Once evolution gave mankind that ability, it was only a matter of time before human subconscious minds began producing feelings that changed their focus from the present to the future. As a consequence, at some point thousands of years ago, people became possessed by the desire to control their own personal futures. To safeguard the future, the human mind had no choice other than to figure out how to make human behavior predictable. So, humans created systems of laws that prescribe how people should behave, and legal systems to impose them.

It was a gigantic change in human behavior to go from living in the moment to living for the future. But the change has gone unnoticed, ever since, because, to our conscious minds, reality is whatever the feelings produced by our subconscious minds say it is. Thus, if the subconscious mind takes a wrong turn, the conscious mind has no platform, no perspective, no point of view from which to take note of the mistake, much less protest it—regardless of the suffering the mistake causes.

The decision to control the future marked the beginning of mankind's bad trip. In our previous natural life, everything worked out according to evolution's guidance. When living for the future, virtually nothing works out. We have to work for practically everything, even our relationships—particularly our relationships.

When we lived in the moment, we loved the people around us unconditionally, because the most basic fact of life was that we needed each other for survival. Now, in our future-oriented way of life, we depend on institutions and money for survival, thus we love *them* unconditionally.

This switch—from loving people, to loving money and institutions—has profoundly transformed the reality experienced by mankind. Arguably, this is as detrimental to our happiness as the transformation experienced by people suffering from dementia. Clinical dementia is caused by diseased subconscious minds, while illusioned subconscious minds cause "culturally imposed dementia." The life of every civilized person on earth has been afflicted by the illusion that the unknowable future can be made knowable, through the control that instituted law exerts on human life. Because of that illusion, none of us feel or behave like normal human beings. The phrase, "culturally imposed dementia" is a harsh judgement on the cultures in which we modern people live. But I am compelled to use it, because it expresses the depth of my concern about what is happening to us.

On the other hand, the term "culturally imposed" carries with it the idea that there is hope for mankind's recovery. And rightly so! It means that our culture is the problem. It means that there is nothing wrong with us. It means it is possible for us to recover our natural way of life.

The first step is to understand how we got here. How we got here is simple, in concept. It's the result of our languaged minds continually producing feelings that place more significance in the future we imagine, than in the reality we experience. Though what's happened is simple, it's not easy to explain, because modern human minds are inoculated against receiving the information. Trying to explain to the civilized mind that any effort to control the longterm future is a mistake is like trying to explain to a person suffering from dementia why their anger is inappropriate. Adding to the difficulty is the fact that the consequences of having lost our way are profound. Most problematic is the fact that the feelings that move us, as modern people, are utterly alien to the feelings that once inspired all our behaviors, in our natural way of life. These two ways of life—the natural one, and the civilized one we now live—are virtual opposites:

In the civilized world, men have traditionally held the social status. In the natural world, the spiritual authority of sisterhoods reigned supreme.

In the civilized world, success is independence. In the natural world, success was interdependence.

In the civilized world, the payoff for success is material wealth. In the natural world, the payoff for success was spiritual wealth, which is love.

In the civilized world, greed is necessary for any sense of well-being, at all. In the natural world, greed could not possibly exist among us—nor can it in the lives of any other social primate, because it is incompatible with the cooperation needed for a social species to survive.

In the civilized world, states are sovereign. In the natural world, Nature was sovereign. Its all-powerful influence was revealed through the actions of all animate beings—including humans— which were universally inspired by feeling emanating from their souls.

Clearly, we modern humans are not behaving normally. If we were, we would take pleasure in fulfilling our spiritual obligations, by placing the needs of our sisters and brothers above our own. It would be like Christmas all year long. People who are free to do what instincts "tell" them to do have no desire to form lifetime pairbonds, nor do they prefer to live alone.

You see, to realize the purpose for which we were born, we need a body of people to serve—sisters and brothers with whom to live in a state of interdependence. The absence of interdependence in modern life banishes the natural spiritual obligations that once united us so closely. *Without spiritual obligations to fulfill, there is no soul-felt reason for us to exist.* As we scurry through our overscheduled modern lives, fulfilling legal obligations, it's easy to overlook the meaninglessness of our existence. But our souls know, and it hurts. Indeed, as evidenced by the ever-increasing drug usage and suicide rates, being without spiritual obligations can prove fatal.

The above paragraph sets forth the framework of everything this book has to say about mankind's circumstances. This book is about the deleterious effects that living without spiritual obligations imposes on mankind's happiness and sense of wellbeing. It exposes the simple mistake that has forced mankind to live this way. It offers hope that humanity will soon rediscover the wisdom of human nature, and live by it, once again. When that happens, our personal lives will make sense, again. And when enough people regain their spiritual freedom, our species will return to its natural life trajectory.

CHAPTER FOUR

Do we Believe in Our Emotional Nature, or in the Law?

My father, a WWI veteran, succeeded in keeping the family's southwestern Kansas ranching and farming operation together through the Great Depression—no small feat. He went on to expand and make a success of the place in the years that followed. So, he didn't have much time to think about religion or philosophy. But I clearly remember the time he shared his views with me about how important religious principles and moral values are. We were out by the stock watering tank southeast of the house, in the late afternoon. "Without moral values," he said, "we would have no notion of right or wrong, in which case anything could happen."

In those words, he revealed to me the values that have justified the existence of civil rule from its beginnings. When he mentioned morals and values, my father was teaching me to believe in them as the basis for the social order that governs human beings. I realize, now, that a father and son who lived before the dawn of civilization would never have had that conversation. It would have been unnecessary, because order was intrinsic in that natural world. Parents didn't need to teach it to their children, because every human was born with it imprinted on his soul—as we still are, today, though civilization requires us to repress it.

Before civilization, consciousness for humans, or awareness, if you will, had nothing to do with culturally imposed understandings— only with actual experience. Every minute was new, for early humans. They actively experienced it, because their psyches were not externally programmed to predefine events according to specific values, such as moral or immoral, good or evil. Such definitions were absent, in natural life, whose metaphor is not judgment, but survival—not obedience to rules written on a wall, but hair-trigger perceptions and responses to the shifting nuances of the immediate situation.

As modern people, the best we seem to be able to do, in terms of living in the moment, is to sit on the edges of our seats at horror movies, reacting with screams and clutching each other at each new harrowing scene. Perhaps the reason horror movies remain so popular is that humans hanker for the sensation of reality that permeates the act of living by perception and response.

Originally, systems of civil rule were based largely on religious beliefs, later, also on secular ones. Different world views. Same result— the belief that humans will run amok, unless governing institutions impose control on their behavior.

Modern humans universally agree with my father that human life would be chaotic, without religiously or legally imposed moral values. But, it's evident that animals don't need them. They simply "know" what to do. Order among the animals is as natural as water flowing downhill. They have no holy books, moral codes, or supreme courts. No rules or laws define elephant families as consisting of sisterhoods and their young, living separately from solitary males. Think of what would happen to the elephant species, if an elephant "empire" arose to dictate that an elephant family unit must consist, instead, of a legally bonded male and female, and their offspring. Would artificially imposed elephant families be functional? Would the elephants be content to live that way? Could their species even continue?

Should we not question the viability of the artificial order we humans have imposed on ourselves, through centralized systems of control? Have we become so dependent on externally imposed order that we moderns can't even imagine life without it?

The facts are clear. Under evolution's natural order—which is inherent, unnoticed, and irrevocable, in natural life—animal life flourished on this planet, for hundreds of millions of years. Prior to civilization, natural human life flourished, also—for 200,000 years, during which all life flourished in the presence of intrinsic, instinctive values. Revealingly, it accomplished this in the *complete absence* of the empires through which humans have since introduced religious and moral values. During our species' 200,000 years of natural life, order among pre-civilized homo sapiens was like the order we can still observe in animals, today. It was as natural as water flowing downhill.

It's different for us, as modern humans. We now live in a world where artificially imposed order is fully entrenched, and maintained by an omnipresent structure of social mores and laws. Laws determine what a family is, not human feelings. They prescribe what each individual is free—or not free—to do. Police forces, legal systems, and prisons enforce the laws. And armies defend the "sovereign states" by whose authority the laws are imposed.

What I am describing, here, is *unnatural* order—an order that our history of failed civilizations clearly indicates is not working for humans, either personally or collectively. As feeling beings, humans are suffering emotionally from the regimentation that defines modern life. Mankind's suffering is now becoming so great, and our future so uncertain, that many thinkers are writing about humankind's potential self-extinction. Given this suffering, how is it possible that humans have never seen their error? But we haven't. Instead, we unfailingly react to the failures of civil states, by creating new civil states—each time thoroughly convinced that we've corrected the mistakes that caused the old regimes to fail.

Until we recognize that the natural order evolution created applies to humans and animals, alike, we humans will never give up on the ideologies and religious beliefs that legitimize mass cultures. For as long as that recognition eludes us, we will have no option but to remain the emotional slaves of the institutional subjugation that has proven so dysfunctional, down through history. We also won't give up on religious and moral beliefs, because they are so crucial to organizing people en masse. For instance, the industrial revolution could not have occurred prior to the existence of mass cultures. But, the material advantages wrought by industrialization fail as a counterbalance to the enormous emotional price we pay for having banished natural order, among humans.

In his book, *Sapiens*, Yuval Noah Harari said that "religion, empires, and money" are the great "unifiers of mankind." What was left unsaid is that, in the process of unifying mankind, humans have obliterated the unconditional love inherent to interdependent relationships, without which natural order cannot exist. Harari went on to say that, "since all social orders and hierarchies are imagined, they are all fragile, and the larger the society, the more fragile it is." His words may one day be the epitaph inscribed on the tombstone of mass civilization.

There are two prices that humanity pays, for the error of subjugating ourselves to legal systems. The immediate price was—and continues to be—the loss of intimacy in our personal relationships. The eventual price is the spectacular collapse of the governments civilized people depend on for survival.

It's time for humankind to recognize that we, too, are subject to natural order—time for a new understanding of what life is about. We need to recognize that it's not the specifics of what the law prescribes as right or wrong that is the problem. The problem is the existence of the law, period! Legal systems separate us from natural order, to which all animate life is, ultimately, subject. Once we realize that, we will inevitably see and accept that human beings are innately guided by the laws of Nature—and that, in Nature, there is room only for natural things.

I realize how difficult it is for modern humans to grasp these concepts that are so foreign to our present way of life. But, facts are facts: Animals have lived among each other far longer than humans, and done so successfully. Knowing that we are alive, and that we are animate beings, how is it difficult to recognize that we, too, are animals, and that evolution has built into every animate being the common sensibilities needed to maintain order? Animals never think about order. They don't have to, because they aren't civilized, thus, are free to be true to how they feel in each moment.

For animals, order is implicit to existence, so much so, that if you asked one how it maintains order, you would, first, have to explain what "order" means. The animal's answer would be, "I just do what I feel like doing. If I feel hungry, I eat. If I feel like loving, I love. If I feel lonely, I find others to be with. If I feel angry, I express my anger. And if I feel the need to share, sacrifice, or kill, then, I share, sacrifice, or kill."

If we humans were free to be true to our emotional nature, our lives, too would be orderly, without ever needing to give any thought to what's right or wrong.

Through instincts, every being "knows" everything there is to know about species' survival—even when to sacrifice or to kill. If we were spiritually free, like the animals, we too would care only about satisfying our feelings. To be true to our emotional nature is to be emotionally as-one with life. This is the ultimate state of ecstasy for any animate being. But, we moderns are not spiritually free. Our current way of life is foreign to our emotional nature, thus, we seldom, if ever, know the ecstasy of losing ourselves in our relationships with the people around us.

As civilized beings, we spend our lives trying to satisfy legal obligations, mostly by making money. Success gets us food and shelter, and maybe even a mansion on the hill, if things go well. But, nothing that can be purchased will ever connect us to life, through unconditional love.

We know we have feelings, but, because we depend on legal systems to maintain order, we've never bothered to figure out why. In our view, the only thing feelings do is stir up trouble, by causing us to break promises, break rules, break even the law, in some cases. In reaction to these "failures," we have become possessed by the belief that we are born sinners, and that our feelings are our enemies, because they cause us to sin. Ironically, this further justifies our belief in the laws that subjugate us—the belief that people will be good, only if forced to.

What a contemptible view to have of ourselves. It costs us dearly, for it has forced us to outlaw the wisdom of human nature on which our ability to love one another, and our species' survival, both depend.

Though evolution has genetically predisposed humans to treat each other in ways that ensure our species' success, the record of human history is rife with examples of humans committing atrocities. This contradiction in our social behavior causes us to believe that human nature has a "dark side." But, does it? It's true that, throughout the history of civilization, soldiers have dutifully obeyed when governments ordered them to commit such atrocities as torture, genocide, and the decimation of indigenous cultures. They did so, not because it was in their nature to harm people who had not offended them, personally, but because institutions—not human nature—ruled their lives. As institutional subjects, people have no option other than to obey. We obey the dictates of institutions, in order to be socially acceptable, to maintain our legal and economic station, and to avoid prison, or, in some instances, even execution.

This so-called dark side of humanity is just one of the many perversities that institutional subjugation thrusts upon all modern human beings—one that has puzzled mankind for centuries. But there's no real mystery involved. People fail to grasp that it is legal subjugation that compels people to commit inhumane acts, not human nature. The unfortunate result is that it causes us to redouble our belief that rules and laws are necessary to protect us from one another. This eventually results in even more inhumane acts.

There seems to be no limit to the depravity of which institutionally subjugated people are capable. For me, the crucifixion of Jesus is *the quintessential example* of how far civilized people are willing to go, for the sake of maintaining civil order.

The story of Jesus' life implies that he orchestrated his own crucifixion. I believe he went to the cross with intent—to awaken us to the mindless behavior imposed on mankind by legal subjugation. When he was brought before the government, he refused to acknowledge it as sovereign, claiming there was another power that was greater. Thus, he literally forced the government to crucify him f*or the "crime" of being human*—being true to the wisdom of his own soul.

Jesus went to the cross, but not to save mankind, as Christianity teaches. He died on the cross to awaken us to the absurdity of our circumstances, *so we could save ourselves.* His sacrifice demonstrates the mindlessness that institutional subjugation imposes on all civilized people—from the leaders who order the killing, to the populace which demands it, to the soldiers who are duty bound to carry it out.

Jesus's sacrifice demonstrates how institutional subjugation warps our nature-given sensibilities, to the point that we will kill a man, like him, for the sake of civil order. I believe there will come a time when people finally recognize that. Then, I believe, they will relieve themselves of institutional dependence, to again embrace each other as sisters and brothers, in spiritual homes where they depend on one another to survive. By doing so, they will save their emotional lives and attain the spiritual authority to stand up against institutional subjugation.

It's one thing to kill a man, like Jesus, who refused to surrender his spiritual authority when instructed by the state: Institutions have no choice other than to do that. But, it's quite another thing to kill a body of women and men who love one another, as a result of trusting their relationships to spiritual obligations. Furthermore, in the act of participating in the life of a *spiritual home*, people will expose the lie upon which civilization is founded—the lie that the human spirit is untrustworthy.

If we humans are to regain access to the wisdom of our own souls, at some point we have to start believing in our own emotional natures. When we do that, we will again be possessed by the desire to become the agents of life we were born to be. It's my view that our spiritual awakening, our salvation, our happiness, and our species' ability to get back on track rest on one thing—that we recognize the centrality of feelings in human existence, thus understand the need to surrender our designs on the future. Then, to love and to be loved, we will base our relationships on spiritual obligations, regardless of how glorious and certain the future promised by legal obligations may seem.

CHAPTER FIVE

Feelings

We need to help our children to become more and more aware that what is essential in life is invisible to the eye.

–Fred (Mister) Rogers

We know why arms and legs exist. That's easy to figure out. Feelings are quite a different thing. They can't be seen, only experienced. Though there is no physical evidence for feelings, they play a crucial role in every facet of human existence—even in consciousness, itself. It's not possible to know what life is about, without recognizing what feelings are about.

Modern humans do not know why feelings exist. *How could we?* To survive, we must honor systems of laws whose *only* concern is appearances. Governments, for instance, don't care about whether married couples are happy. Their only concern is that they are not physically abusing one another, and that they honor the contract of marriage, for life. To me, Mr. Roger's message is for adults, even more than for children. We need to help one another "to become more and more aware that what is essential in life is invisible to the eye."

So, why are feelings, though invisible, so essential in life? As it happens, the answer dawns easily, once we ask the right question.

Curiously, it is one that mankind has never asked. Q: "What would life be like with no feelings to satisfy, no desires to fulfill?" A: If there were no desires to satisfy, no one would have anything to do. There would be no activities for the rational mind to evaluate when deciding on how to best satisfy feelings, thus no evidence of consciousness, at all. *In essence, it is our desires—our feelings—that are the very stuff of consciousness. Feelings are the values which underlie every reasoned choice we make.*

Thousands of years ago, our forbearers made a huge mistake, by overruling feelings with laws. Lawmakers acted out of ignorance, when they forced people to survive by being true to laws, rather than allowing them the freedom to serve life, by being true to their feelings. At the time, mankind was unaware that people can neither be happy nor true to life, without feelings to satisfy—a failure of insight that remains with us to this day.

Here is another—even more fundamental—question that mankind has never asked. "Why do feelings exist?" Once one understands the significance of feelings, it becomes clear that they are there to inspire the behaviors required for the perpetuation of life.

I believe our failure to understand why feelings exist has everything to do with the myriad problems that plague mankind. Think of the dysfunctional family relationships from which humans chronically suffer, the ever-increasing drug usage and suicide rates, and the divide between people of different political persuasions that is so great it prevents them from agreeing on *anything!* Then, consider the stockpiles of weapons deployed to defend ideologies and institutions. If that's not enough, overarching it all are environmental problems that threaten to denature the planet.

To resolve these problems, we need to regain access to the wisdom of human nature, which humans have shunned since we first subjugated ourselves to culturally imposed moral edicts. The only access we have to that wisdom is our feelings—the very feelings we are trying to ignore when we beseech each other not to allow feelings to affect our decisions.

Why have we humans adapted a way of life in which we are rebuked—and even rebuke ourselves—each time we allow feelings to influence our decisions? The cause is our modern human way of life, and the belief on which it is based—that the future must, at all costs, be controlled. Our obsession with the future prevents us from acknowledging the wisdom of our souls, which is there to inform us about how to react to the situation at hand—not how to control the unknowable future.

There was a time, very long ago, when humans did not try to control the future. Back then, all obligations were spiritual ones, based on our innate desires. By contrast, modern humans associate success and happiness, and *even survival,* with realizing *future* objectives. As a result, our obligations—including family ones—are legal, not spiritual.

Legal obligations aren't based on our innate desire to help each other survive, but on each individual's desire to realize the objective of a certain future. So, when *we* ask, "What if I do this? What if I do that?" we choose the behavior that we think will most likely satisfy a specific *objective*. In instances where our *desire* to realize a certain future conflicts with our *desire* to satisfy an innately based feeling, such as romance, we choose to satisfy the objective over the natural feeling, regardless of how much we suffer, as a result of that choice. We think of this as self-discipline, when, in truth, it constitutes spiritual repression. And it *always* hurts, no matter which natural feeling we are choosing to deny.

We moderns don't realize it, but our unnatural state of suffering is a result of devoting our entire lives to the objective of realizing a certain future. We behave as though we are oblivious to the resulting emotional pain. But we feel it, nonetheless. Indeed, the suffering is so omnipresent that the first of the four noble truths of Buddhism is: Life is suffering, for which relief comes through meditation, and various other practices. Christians, on the other hand, find relief in the belief that there will be no suffering in the afterlife, or that suffering will end when their savior returns.

In all such cases, the actual problem is missed, entirely, because, as subjects of a system of laws that require constant self-discipline, we continually have to lie about how we feel, in order to realize those all-important future objectives. Unbeknownst to us, however, real damage is being done, because each lie is a refutation of life, itself. This directly harms our emotional wellbeing, and we suffer. It doesn't matter whether we believe in religion, institutions, ideology, science, technology, or progress: When we aren't free to experience the comfort of being true to our feelings of the moment, we have little choice other than take what comfort we can in the anticipation of the future happiness that is promised by these beliefs.

How ironic it is that, in our world, which gives us no choice but to live for the future, beliefs that cannot be verified are essential to our emotional health. (If the promise of beliefs were verifiable, we would not refer to them as beliefs.) Because we are suffering, we have a clear need to understand the cause-and-effect that is occurring in our lives: Every time we try to control the future, we unknowingly disconnect ourselves from the wisdom of our souls, a wisdom which has no designs on the distant future. Our souls have been accumulating wisdom since the first stirrings of life on earth—long enough to know that future certainty doesn't exist, for the obvious reason that the future is unknowable. Our souls would never engage us in such pointless pursuits as trying to control the future. They wouldn't, because they share Jesus's perspective:

Take care of one another, now. Let the future take care of itself.

The very nature of civilization is what threw us off course. In civilization, legal obligations must be fulfilled, for the sake of civil order, which is the reason Jesus had to be eliminated. We moderns do not realize that the constraints legal obligations place on the human spirit, leave none of us free to honor the wisdom of our souls—the normal human way of taking care of one another, *now*. Sometimes, as in the wake of earthquakes, hurricanes, and other natural disasters, civil order temporarily breaks down and, suddenly, our spirits get a "get-out-of-jail-free" card. For awhile, they are free to reveal the sensibilities that evolution built into each of us. It's at these times that we find news anchors closing their evening broadcasts with examples of how our humanity shines, in times of disorder. We fail to realize that such temporary anomalies of behavior are telling us something important—that our souls are still intact, that they still speak to us.

But, the reconnection, unfortunately, is brief. When "normalcy" is restored, our subconscious minds immediately refocus our conscious ones on realizing future objectives, and our humanity is no longer part of the scene. One might say it's as if our spirits have gone to sleep, again. But, why wouldn't our spirits sleep? They have no responsibilities—nothing to do—in a world in which order is based on legal obligations.

There are, of course, occasions when human spirits *do* revolt against institutional subjugation. Spiritual revolt comes in many forms, from divorce and domestic violence to civil disobedience and insurrection—all of which the civilized mind categorizes as "human failings." Revolt, in the context of civilization, is futile, regardless of its scope. The grip that institutions and their rules have on human minds is far too strong. Instead of recognizing civil disorder for what it is—the revolt of our spirits against the system—we interpret it as the ill-intended, sinful, evil, uncaring acts of inadequate people.

So, to avoid being judged as an "evil" or "inadequate" person, our spirit mostly sleeps, or inspires us to take comfort in beliefs, dreams, or drugs, to counter the pain of spiritual repression. That is how things are in the modern world. But it's not how Nature "designed" things to be.

The following quotation reveals the consequences of subjugating our lives to legal obligations:

> *Race, Religion, Nationality, Gender, Status.*
> *In our darkest moments we don't see our differences.*
> *In our darkest moments our humanity shines brightly.*
> *Why do we only wake up in the dark?*
>
> —Global Dignity Day Quote

Now we have the answer. What we moderns see as our darkest moments are actually the brightest ones, for our spirits. Those are the moments when we are free to fulfill our spiritual obligations—the moments when our humanity comes to the fore and we reach out to take care of one another. What societal rules and laws cause us to see as our "darkest moments" are actually the happiest ones for our spirits, because it's during those moments that we become cognizant of our need, of our love, for one another.

Perhaps it's time for us to ask why our spirits can't be free all the time—to do what Nature designed them to do. Maybe we should try to understand how we were disconnected from our spirits, and with the happiness that flows freely, when we honor the wisdom of our souls. It is our own nature that is rebelling, because Nature will not be denied. Our spirits will never stop calling for us to reclaim the life into which humanity was born, and in which all obligations are spiritual, none legal.

I firmly believe we *can* reclaim our natural way of life, with one caveat: We can't accomplish it by doing what modern humans always do—making it another objective. We can accomplish it by, once again, being true to the wisdom of our souls. Do that, and it will occur naturally. There is one prerequisite for that: Before we can be true to our souls, we have to rediscover the wisdom of human nature. This book has been written to facilitate that rediscovery.

Rediscovery is essential, because the problem we face is civilization, itself. We have grown up steeped in its assumptions, and in the thrall of the institutions of civil rule that have made it possible for humans to live in mass cultures. The result of mass civilization is the world of conveniences we enjoy, but, it is becoming ever more evident that those conveniences do not satisfy the needs of our souls, and that our institutions cannot deliver the peaceful, just futures they promise. We suffer alienation in our personal lives—and suffer also from the nagging sense that all systems of justice are fatally flawed. Yet we continue to go along with them—even worship them—in the hope that they will eventually make good on their word. We accept the flawed reality institutions impose, not because we are satisfied with it, but because it's the only game in town, and it's gone on so long that no one knows what to do about it.

To break out of this paradigm, and get our lives back on track, we need to recognize how legal obligations blind us to our spiritual ones. Recognition will free us to embrace our natural human way of being, in which success is the result of behaving according to how we naturally feel like behaving, not by subjugating ourselves to the impositions of moral laws.

CHAPTER SIX

How Things Are vs. How we Believe they Should Be

A few weeks after entering the first grade, my nephew, Nathan, left school, one day, and told his parents he was never going back. "Why?," his parents asked. Nathan's answer: "Because I don't want to." The school principal was called, and soon all three adults were asking, "Why don't you want to go to school?" "I don't have to answer that question," Nathan replied.

From Nathan's perspective, as a six-year-old boy who had not yet been indoctrinated in the ways of this world, the situation was as simple as this: If I told you I was hungry, or that I don't like being lost in a blizzard, or that a sunset is beautiful, or that I love you, you wouldn't ask me to explain it. "Why are you asking me to explain why I don't like school?"

Like all other animate beings, we humans come into the world expecting that satisfying our feelings of the moment is ample justification for our behavior. In other words, because feelings tell us how things are, they don't need explanation. I believe this is what Jesus meant when he said, "To enter heaven, we must come as little children."

In voicing his expectation that he didn't have to go to school, because he didn't feel like going, Nathan became the voice of the human spirit, the voice of Christ—a voice whose message runs counter to everything the modern world teaches. To succeed in *our* world, we are taught to pursue objectives—not to honor the feelings evolution handed down to us.

There are profound reasons for a young boy not to like school, and we ignore them all when we indoctrinate him to the point that he feels he has no choice but to go. They include: being separated from loved ones; having to sit still and contained for hours; and, eventually, having to establish an identity independent of the natural one provided by home and family. And then, the ultimate spiritual insult—being forced to learn abstract material in which he has no inherent interest, and then being publicly classified as a success or failure, based on his proficiency at doing so.

To a mind that has not been indoctrinated in the ways of this world, formal education is best described as the punishment civilized people get for being born. The immediate consequence of our indoctrination is emotional pain, a pain Nathan had to endure throughout his school years. Emotional pain is so disruptive to the human spirit that I believe it is the reason so many states are introducing classes on emotional health in their elementary schools. In a news program, a teacher was shown asking her students: How many of you are suffering from anxiety? The whole class raised their hands. What a blessing for those children to know, at least, that they are not alone. The governor of Arizona recently announced a twenty million dollar increase in school budgets, to provide counselors to deal with the "epidemic of social and emotional disconnection, depression, and suicide in our public schools."

The ultimate consequences of allowing ourselves to be subjugated to the emotional insults of the classroom, and countless other institutional requirements, are evident throughout the world of adults all around us, who spend most of their time doing things in which they have no emotional investment. In effect, it is a world populated by people who are spiritually sleepwalking through life.

All spiritual sleepwalkers think their behavior is exclusively rational. But, knowing that all behavior is driven by the need to satisfy feelings, we must question whether it is rational for a worker to arise early each morning and fight traffic, in order to get to work on time to do a job he doesn't feel like doing. If he were being true to his feelings of the moment, the feelings of his soul, it wouldn't be rational. He would never do it. However, if he is doing it because he *feels* that he doesn't want to end up homeless, then "living for the future" is the only behavior that *is* rational. To be spiritually alive, however, requires that we be alive to our feelings of the moment, not "alive" to concerns about the distant future.

The fact is, we are being *spiritually dishonest* every time we do things we don't like to do, because of concerns about what our circumstances may be years from now. This is the definition of spiritual dishonesty, which results in spiritual death, a condition so commonplace in our institutionalized world that we don't realize it's happening. The point, again, is that all behavior is the result of the need to satisfy feelings. In the natural world, those feelings are directly connected to our instincts. In the institutionalized world, feelings are artificially redirected toward concerns about how we intend to survive an unknowable future—a big difference.

Feelings are the motivation for all behavior, and there are two distinct kinds. Feelings that are instinctive arise directly from our souls. Feelings based on beliefs are byproducts of our hope to realize objectives in the future. These two kinds of feelings are easy to distinguish:

Feelings based on instinct are self-evident. They *cannot be argued with,* because they tell us how things are, as in "I am cold," "I am hungry," "I am angry," "I am lonely," or "I am falling in love." Feelings based on beliefs, however, *can be endlessly argued with* such as our belief in an ideology, institution, or religion. Feelings based on beliefs do not represent how things *are,* but how we believe things *should be.*

Whenever we deny a feeling based on instinct, in favor of one inspired by what we've been taught about how things should be, we are ignoring the voice of the human spirit, Nathan's voice, Christ's voice, and we suffer.

All people who are subject to instituted law suffer, in this way, because they must ignore the voice of the human spirit, for the sake of their survival, just as Nathan had to deny his own innate sensibilities to manage *his* situation. As a consequence of ignoring our real feelings, mankind is, in effect, floating about in a cloud connected to nothing that's real. Instead of acknowledging the reality through which our instincts tell us how things are, we value the promises of our beliefs, as if *they* are real.

"Be careful what you wish for, lest you get it." The promises of beliefs are not real, in that the futures they promise cannot satisfy our soul-felt needs, even if the promise is realized. As subjects of civil rule, we are participating in a confidence game that can continue only for as long as the populace holds common beliefs—common illusions. We keep playing the game, but, not because we *really* believe in it. It's because our minds accept as real whatever we must do to survive.

But, our spiritual needs—which we must attend to, in order to know real contentment—can be satisfied only when participating in an intimate culture based on spiritual trust. Consequently, civil states eventually, and unequivocally, fail, all for the same reason. Increasing discontent within the populace eventually causes people to begin losing confidence in the rules that govern the game. Then, people start believing in opposing rules, or ideologies, about how to change things so the culture *will* work. But, the problem is the confidence game, itself. There is no solution. The end finally comes when opposing viewpoints are expressed with guns, instead of words.

The consequence of living in cultures created and sustained by beliefs about what should be, is starkly evident in the inability of political opponents to communicate with each other. This is not a failure of intelligence, reason, or of caring. What makes sense in one belief-based reality is senseless in the other. From evolutionary wisdom's perspective, all belief-based realities are senseless. But, the spirits of institutionally subjugated people are so repressed, that no one is able to care.

The point of all this is: If you took the most drastic political, ideological, or religious opponents—including terrorists—and dropped them into an intimate natural human culture where everyone is dependent on each other to survive, they would instantly have each other's backs. The human spirit always takes over whenever humans are in interdependent relationships in the context of survival. It knows everything there is to know about species survival and about love. But the power of all its wisdom gets lost—indeed, turns on itself—when people live in mass cultures that force them to accept the promises of beliefs, as truths, in order to survive.

In a TV interview about a comment President Obama once made about the "danger of the cancel culture," Jenna Bush asked Michelle Obama, "What do you say to people who want to be closer to each other?" I felt Mrs. Obama's response revealed how common are the sensibilities possessed by the human spirit. She replied: "I had an opportunity to sit by your father (President George Bush) at a funeral, and we shared stories about our kids and about our parents. Our values are the same. We disagree on policy. But we don't disagree on humanity. We don't disagree about love and compassion. I think that's true for all of us. It's just that we get lost in our fears of what's different."

Given Mrs. Obama's response, one can't help but wonder how humanity could possibly avoid getting lost in the fears of what's different, in a world governed by policy. Our brains didn't evolve to create policy. As creations of Life, creations of Nature, we didn't evolve to know how to live by such dictates. So, no, it's not surprising at all that—over issues of policy—we have become, first spiritual enemies, and eventually, blood enemies.

Wouldn't it be remarkable if we could return to the way things really are—a world without policy? The world into which mankind was born was without either beliefs or fear of the future, a life in which humans are as spiritually alive to the moment as are all other living beings. Is that even possible for us, anymore?

Yes, it *is* possible for us to be spiritually alive, again, because our instincts are still intact—as were Nathan's, as evident by his insistence that he didn't have to go to school, because he didn't want to. In other words, he was acting on his feelings. If formal education existed to serve the life of our species, Nathan would have loved going to school. Unfortunately, it exists, instead, to teach children how to survive an ideologically based way of life, and how to serve the state on which that way of life depends. It is because formal education does not serve life that Nathan's innate wisdom—still intact—made going to school such an unpleasant experience, for him. Some children like school, of course, but that's probably because it's one of the few places modern humans can associate as the social primates we are. At least girls get to hang out with girls, and boys with boys, just as females hung out with females, and males with males, throughout human and pre-human evolution.

Yes, we can regain our spiritual lives. To do so, we must journey back from the imagined future, where we now live, to the only way of life in which we can again be alive to the moment. The first step is to understand how we humans originally made the mistake of creating a world in which reality is based on how we believe things should be, not on how they are. If we can understand this, as sure as thunder follows lightning, we will stop participating in the mistake. We will form "spiritual homes," again—the kind in which people are bonded, in spiritual trust. When participating in the life of a *real human family*, the key to survival is spiritual honesty—being true to how we feel in the moment.

A spiritual home is the central feature of natural human life. It is the human social unit, or survival unit. It is the natural human family that nurtures spiritually free human life. It is the extended family, made up of sisterhoods and brotherhoods which bond all members into a viable, self-perpetuating whole. When modern humans return to spiritual homes, they will experience the contentment inherent to mankind's natural way of life. Even we moderns will experience this contentment, immediately. This sense of comfort, reassurance, and wellbeing is so contagious that such homes would spread quickly, once re-introduced. Spiritual freedom—the freedom to be true to what is, instead of to the way we believe things should be—would soon take on a life of its own.

CHAPTER SEVEN

Living in Denial of our Emotional Intelligence

They kiss, they hold hands, they swagger, they shake their fist, the kinds of things we do, and they do them in the same context. They have very sophisticated cooperation when they hunt, and they share the prey. They show emotions that we describe has happiness, sadness, fear. They have a sense of humor... the kinds of things that traditionally have been thought of as human prerogatives.

—Jane Goodall

Researchers like Diane Fossey and Jane Goodall, who have spent extensive time with social primates in the wild, have discovered that sensibilities such as empathy, compassion, and altruism, which humans had long thought were exclusive to our species, are richly present among our cousins in the wild.

In short, we *are* animals, like our social primate cousins. But, because we live by moral laws, we believe ourselves to be on a higher moral plane, even though, from our soul's perspective, nothing has changed: Our emotional make-up remains that of a social species dependent on intimate, interdependent relationships, for happiness and contentment. Evolution honed us for this, and it is because of evolution that, if the animal in us is not content, then we are not content, nor are we taking care of life. As subjects of moral laws, we are not free to satisfy our animal needs. Hence, our growing dissatisfaction with our lives and the increasingly deep scar we are leaving upon the earth. Animals do not destroy their habitats.

This book introduces the philosophy that I call Spiritual Freedom, which springs from my belief that human life would naturally organize itself, if people were free to be true to how they feel. Spiritual Freedom flows from the idea that humans, like all other animate beings, inherit an emotional intelligence through which we instinctively know how to react to every given situation, in a way that serves the life of our species. When spiritually free—not subject to legally imposed notions of what's right or wrong—our way of life serves life, and we naturally find contentment and happiness in that service.

From this book's perspective, emotional intelligence is essential for any species to flourish. Emotional intelligence always guided us, from the birth of our species, until we were subjugated by civilization. Legal subjugation changed everything. As a result of civil rule, mankind now worships reason to the point that we completely ignore the guidance of our emotions. Indeed, we see our ability to reason as the beginning and end of all things.

The idea that emotions provide the guidance needed for species' survival fundamentally challenges the traditional philosophical thought on which the modern world turns. It turns on the legal systems that mankind created—albeit with the best of intentions—to provide a rational way to maintain order, among humans. But, those systems only provide the appearance of order. As a result, modern humans place infinitely more value on the appearance of order than its unintended consequence—the emotional suffering we experience from being subject to such shallow and fragile notions of order.

The power of reason is further venerated in the modern mind by our advances in science and technology. But, as the products wrought by these advances rain down on us in torrents, it's becoming increasingly clear that these goods, remarkable though they are, have little to do with happiness. Quite the opposite. They are driving us, and our children, crazy. Even worse, the environmental issues caused by producing our modern marvels are so alarming that people now argue for increased space exploration, in the belief that our species will soon need another home.

Granted, reason—of which all animate beings are capable—combined with mankind's unique linguistic skills, has empowered humans to achieve remarkable things. But there's something reason can never do: It cannot inspire individuals to behave in ways that perpetuate the cycle of life. Only emotional intelligence can do that!

Traditional philosophic thought represents mankind's effort to provide a rational explanation for life's purpose and meaning. It posits the idea that, via the power of pure reason, mankind will eventually be able to explain everything. From the perspective of spiritual freedom, however, there is no explanation for life's meaning. Life's meaning is experienced as a feeling. Like any other emotion, life's meaning can't be explained, only felt.

For me to attempt to explain life's meaning from a rational point of view would be like Copernicus or Galileo using the accepted precepts of their day to explain their discoveries about how the solar system is organized. Because there is no rational explanation for life's meaning, it's quite natural that humans find significance in our belief that mankind is at the center of things. It's difficult, therefore, for people to grasp *any* idea that is not human-centric. Back in Copernicus's time, it was "stepping-off-a-cliff shocking" for people to let go of the idea that we did not live at the center of the universe—despite the idea's simplicity. In their search for meaning, philosophers and theologians quite naturally attempt to explain the human condition from the perspective that our existence is special, relative to the overall scheme of things. Little wonder that astronauts were astonished when they observed the earth from outer space, on their journeys to the moon.

I realized suddenly how insignificant we all are. We're just tucked away in space around a rather normal star, the sun—probably just one of billions of stars in the universe. I personally thought that everybody would like to have that view as we did, to see the earth as it really is.

—Jim Lovell, Astronaut

The concept of spiritual freedom is life-centric, *not* human-centric, thus it calls into question the entirety of traditional philosophical thought. To understand the human condition from the perspective of spiritual freedom, we need to cleanse ourselves of the idea that our existence has a special significance—as individuals or as a species.

Why would I bother people with such a disquieting idea? Because, in order to talk about reality, we have to start with what's real, regardless of how profoundly people don't want to hear it. Copernicus was so concerned about people's reaction to the fact that we don't live at the center of the universe that he withheld his manuscript from publication until shortly before his death. Even then, it was published in another country, by a friend who lived there. People were also offended by Galileo's revelations—so much so that he was put under house arrest, and forced to stop talking about it for the duration of his life.

The behavior of those who rejected Copernicus's and Galileo's revelations illustrates how tightly the brain "circles the wagons" around its beliefs. It protects its illusions from reality by subconsciously rejecting any and all evidence that does not comply with them. When our sense of identity and wellbeing is grounded in a belief—whether the ancient belief that mankind lived at the center of the universe, or the current belief that mankind's existence is special—our minds have no choice, but to reject all evidence that contradicts what they believe. They must continue to believe, in order to prevent the mind-body from entering a state of shock. Thus, beliefs are not based on objective evidence. They exist because they are essential to our emotional health, when we're not free to experience the satisfaction that results when being true to our emotions in our service to life.

How significant *is* the existence of mankind in the overall scheme of things? Well, the planet was doing fine before humans existed. Why wouldn't it continue to do well, without us? Furthermore, had the dinosaurs not been wiped out by a massive meteor impact, tens of millions of years ago, mammals would never have gained the dominance they have, in which case homo-sapiens wouldn't exist, now, anyway. Regarding the individual existence of any of us: If our mother had not met our father—an improbability that is compounded with each generation—you or I would not exist. Or, if one sperm out of the tens of millions seeking to fertilize the egg had succeeded, other than the one that did, our brother or sister would be here, not us.

Our mother would have loved our brother or sister, just as she loved us. We wouldn't have been missed by our own mother. If our mother wouldn't have missed us, what chance is there that the universe would?

From the point of view of Spiritual Freedom, it becomes evident that *the organizing principle of animate life is as elemental and impersonal as the laws of physics that govern the trajectories of heavenly bodies.* The core value of this organizing principle, expressed entirely and exclusively through genetically encoded emotions, is that the cycle of life shall continue. Like other living beings on this planet, all humans are born with the emotional intelligence necessary to guide them in performing their natural role of sustaining life. It's quite natural, therefore, that our lives feel real only when we are serving our evolutionarily assigned role—a role our would-be brother or sister would otherwise have served.

This bears repeating: We only feel real when doing things that serve life. *The "real human self" finds fulfillment in serving life through attending the needs of others. There is no such thing as self-realization*, because no one can find fulfillment through serving self. If we feel unfulfilled, it's because we exist without the spiritual obligations inherent to sisterhoods and brotherhoods. The human organism emotionally craves, above all else, the connectedness that comes exclusively from serving others, in relationships of mutual dependence. One's life cannot be realized in a spiritual vacuum, no matter how expansive or well-outfitted the physical circumstances.

Given how long mankind has suffered from spiritual estrangement, it's not surprising that all philosophies focus on the concept of self-realization—the antithesis of connectedness. Indeed, we accept the promise of religions, ideologies, institutions, and laws in the belief that, by adhering to their precepts or dictates, we can serve self. These self-serving beliefs are the building blocks of the spiritual travesty that is modern civilization. Little wonder that mankind is plagued with unhappiness, loneliness, and anxiety.

Consider the following thoughts:

We come into the world needing others.
Then we are told it's braver to go it alone.
That independence is the way to accomplish.

But there's another way to live.
A way that sees the only path to fulfillment is through others.

That our time here can be deep beyond measure.

No one who chose interdependence ever found despair.
Because what the world taught as weakness,
Is in fact our greatest virtue.

In my search for the author of those words, all I could find was: "perennial wisdom." That's poetic, in itself. It implies that every human being values, and has always valued, the sentiments implicit in those words. Yet, by extolling independence, our way of life forces us to ignore their implications, for the sake of our self-respect, if not our survival.

There is an urgent need for humans to understand why we have chosen a way of life that virtually guarantees we will live in denial of our emotional intelligence. For too long, we have been prisoners of our universal belief that the future must be controlled. We invented the legal systems that govern us, as tools for securing our personal needs, for life. But their very existence sentences us to devoting our entire lives to taking care of ourselves, alone. Having to live in denial of our inborn need to serve others leave us emotionally lost and confused.

From the perspective of our souls, we are here for one reason. We are not here for self-aggrandizement, or to realize future objectives, or to make the world a better place. We are here to participate in the process of life that has been going on for hundreds of millions of years. As modern humans, we have not participated in that process for thousands of years. Only when we are again free to serve others in relationships of mutual dependence will *our time here again be deep beyond measure.*

Everyone knows what makes people happy—and it isn't wealth and privilege. It is the depth of our connections to the people around us. That's no mystery. The mystery is that humans have chosen an institutionalized way of life, which obliterates those connections. By looking at the human condition from the perspective of spiritual freedom, I hope to demystify how and why that happened.

To succeed in our modern world, we must deny our moment-to-moment feelings, every time they conflict with our lifetime plans—especially in our relationships. Unbeknownst to us, doing so constitutes "emotional dishonesty," and it breaks our natural connections to one another—connections which are essential to our ability to experience life's meaning. Regardless of how materially privileged or educated we may be, these numerous self-denials, spiritual dishonesties, and unhealthy focus on an unknowable future keep us emotionally isolated, disoriented, and bewildered. This explains why drug addiction, "belief addiction," difficult familial relationships, loneliness, depression, anxiety, and increasing suicide rates do not respect social or economic boundaries.

If only we could understand why—with the best of intentions—our predecessors long ago chose a way of life that placed us at crosspurposes with our inborn sensibilities. Then, in search of a meaningful existence, we would surely look deep within ourselves, and find our real selves, as Nature made them. We would let *them* point the way to the life that comes naturally to humans—a way of life in which being emotionally honest and living in the moment are keys to *both our happiness and our species survival.*

If we *were* serving life, right now, all would be different. We would feel immersed in life's significance, as though we were living at the very center of all there is. We would be special, not in the eyes of God or the universe, but in each other's eyes. Time would stand still, because we would be engaged exclusively in the moment. We would be free to satisfy our emotional hungers, *as* they occur, thus would have no need to seek deferred fulfilment in the hereafter, or in promises, dreams, or beliefs. We would have no concern about how the universe is organized—much less whether or not we lived at its center. If we were being true to our emotional intelligence, rather than living in denial of it, there would be no need for philosophers, theologians, or mystics to explain life's meaning. When we are free to be true to the wisdom of our souls, we perpetually experience life's purpose and meaning, and significance is implicit.

CHAPTER EIGHT

Evolutionary Wisdom—Not Accumulated Knowledge—is the Source of Happiness

We are drowning in information while starving for wisdom.

—E. O. Wilson, Evolutionary Biologist

We live in a modern world where we seek happiness in accumulated knowledge. We believe that knowledge, and the myriad products it makes possible—such as fancier cars, flying from New York to London faster, a smarter phone, and robots in our kitchens—will make us happier. In that belief, we overlook the fact that mankind is an anxiety ridden species, despite all our modern marvels. In truth, none of these products have anything to do with happiness—an assertion that needs no further support beyond the fact that modern people are increasingly dissatisfied with the lives we live.

The fact is, we are social primates. Written in our emotional heritage—in our very nature, as living beings—is the fact that we humans can only be happy through deep emotional connections with the people around us. Accumulated knowledge enables us to secure our material needs. But, despite how materially well off we are, there can be no real contentment for human beings, without the connection to life that comes exclusively through our love for others.

Our modern world disconnected us from the intimacy inherent to interdependent relationships by controlling human behavior through moral law. This turned off the spigot of contentment and happiness that naturally flows when humans are being true to life. Every individual is born genetically programmed to experience pleasure in the behaviors that have proven over eons to best serve the species.

It's no accident that evolution is as much about happiness as it is about the survival of the species. Think of the pleasure we take in feelings of romance—the motivator for procreation. Think of the pleasure and excitement groups of men experience, when facing danger—the result of their innate motivation to protect others who carry their genes. Think, too, of the pleasure a mother experiences when nurturing the child who carries her genes. Mothers even take pleasure in dying for their children, if things come to that.

These are salient examples of how evolution sees to it that the genes most likely to be handed down are the ones of individuals who most love doing the things that enhance the species' ability to flourish. Such individuals—male or female—are the better caretakers, providers and protectors. If, by chance, they die in that service, others who carry their genes will further enhance the group's genetic code, by handing down the predisposition to naturally take pleasure in behaviors that serve life. As a result of eons of such genetic selection, all animate beings are emotionally predisposed to find happiness doing the things that take care of life. Indeed, from evolution's perspective, *there is no higher state of mind than happiness.*

"When I was 5 years old, my mother always told me that happiness was the key to life. When I went to school, they

asked me what I wanted to be when I grew up. I wrote down 'happy'. They told me I didn't understand the assignment, and I told them they didn't understand life."

—John Lennon

The greatest pleasure evolution affords humans—beyond romance and motherly love—is sisterly and brotherly love. It's the emotion that brings happiness when women and men cooperate in social groups that serve life. Lennon's mother had it right. Happiness is precisely what life is about. But, Lennon's instructors were stuck in the modern paradigm that was created when humans imposed moral laws to control the future. In our world, happiness is not seen as significant, compared to plans and career. How ironic it is that we modern humans, who believe ourselves so highly evolved, have no access to the unconditional love that is inherent to sisterly and brotherly love.

Without the contentment we were meant to experience, through the intimacy of interdependent relationships, our souls are left to find gratification, somehow. Consequently, we find ourselves seeking contentment where it doesn't really exist. A perfect example of this is our desire to accumulate knowledge. We think that, if we are not happy now, surely with enough knowledge, we'll gain the ability to create even more amazing things, and, someday we will be happy. Civil rule has facilitated the development of this, and many other "band-aids" to sooth our deeply felt need for meaning and contentment, a need that an institutionalized way of life cannot satisfy.

The monetary and legal systems that define civil rule have facilitated the development of mass societies in which people who do not even know each other can cooperate on huge projects—like the CERN particle accelerator in Switzerland, constructed to research the nature of matter. The combined result of such projects is the massive body of information in which modern humans take much pride, and which continues to grow exponentially with the passage of time.

But, from our soul's point of view, our advanced knowledge—including everything from the discovery that the earth is round to the big bang theory, and beyond—has nothing to do with what ultimately matters. What matters to our souls is that we take care of the life of our species, according to our innate sensibilities. The mass of accumulated human knowledge contributes nothing to real contentment, happiness, or the ability to love and be loved.

E. O. Wilson's observation that we are drowning in information, provides a clue to the reason why our species has become a cancerous blight on the face of this planet. Having allowed legal commitments to disconnect us from our innate wisdom, we now seek contentment in information and the progress it makes possible. But, information can't save us from the emotional pain inherent to a spiritually repressed way of life. Our belief that it can, keeps us looking for contentment where it doesn't exist— "looking for love in all the wrong places."

The result of seeking satisfaction in information and progress is an insatiable need for more information and progress. The growth of information is incessant, like that of a cancerous tumor. Having detached ourselves from the wisdom of our souls, on which we normally depend for order, we now base our legal systems on accumulated legal knowledge. Thus, governments utilize knowledge to justify laws that repress our innate sensibilities. This renders us emotionally disfigured in the same way a tumor leaves us physically disfigured.

Call me anti-intellectual, but our love affair with knowledge has resulted in an artificial world that separates us from our origins—from the evolutionary wisdom that yet resides in each of our souls, waiting to be rediscovered. I must declare that there is something fundamentally wrong that endangers both the individual and the species, when we seek contentment in knowledge, while turning our backs on the wisdom of our souls. After all, human knowledge has been accumulating in documents, for only a few thousand years, while the wisdom of our souls has been accumulating in our genes for hundreds of millions of years.

Compared to the information accumulated by modern man, primitive people had very little—no formal education, no universities, no scientific research, and no libraries. They didn't even have a written language. The only information they had was what they and their predecessors learned from experience. Yet, without need for focus or intent, they were able to know the pleasure of sisterly-brotherly love, a state of contentment in which life feels so complete that people have no desire for anything more.

Love is the key element that enables primitive people to live in a state of balance with the natural world. People who experience unconditional love are satisfied with *what is*—whether it comes through romantic love, motherly love, or sisterly-brotherly love. More significantly, they are delighted with it. In other words, only when we humans are again free to be emotionally honest will we know the love that relieves us of our current obsession with ever-more-things—more knowledge, more progress, more technology, etc.

In his book, *Don't Sleep, there are Snakes,* Daniel Everett tells of his inability to convert the primitive Pirahã people to Christianity, after thirty years of trying. The Pirahã are an indigenous people who live deep in the Brazilian rainforest—some of the last people on earth still living as their ancient ancestors did. As do all primitive people, they learn from experience, not words. Everett tried, but could not convert them, he said, because the words of Jesus—a man whom they had never personally experienced—were meaningless to them. In my estimation, another reason he could not convert them is that they were contented, as the result of being spiritually free. Indeed, missionaries and researchers who have spent time with them are quoted as describing the Pirahã as "the happiest people on earth." Note: They have no rules, no money, no laws, no moral edicts, and they don't practice marriage.

The idea of the future never enters the minds of the Pirahã, because they have no investment in it, no plans, no legal edicts, no openended promises. They spend their whole lives invested in the unfolding moment. Living in this state of spiritual honesty, they have no need for Jesus's message. How could they? Having never left Eden, they are living the way of life that Jesus implored us all to live.

It is because they suffer no pain of spiritual repression that they have no need for the promise of beliefs. The Pirahã don't even have an origin or a destiny story! But civilized people need beliefs to cope with the pain of spiritual repression that is inevitable when life is ruled by legal edicts. The best we can do to quell the pain, is to take what comfort we can in the promises of beliefs. This is the reason beliefs are so sacred, to the civilized mind.

The fact that the Pirahã are happy, even though the only information they have is what they learn from experience, begs this question: Why do we moderns need so much knowledge? We need it, because, in our world, each person's survival depends on making money. In *our* world, we need ever-more knowledge, information, education, and accomplishments to make more money. But, acquiring ever-more information only means we can accomplish more things that have nothing to do with why we are here. When, despite all the efforts and accomplishments of mankind, we feel suffused with the sense that our lives are meaningless, it is our souls telling us that our accomplishments have nothing to do with taking care of life, remarkable as they may be.

Our need to make money spawned the industrial revolution, which ushered in a world in which the human spirit isn't needed—only human labor. Since the advent of industrialization, people in modern cultures have functioned largely as robots in service to the captains of industry. Whatever sensibilities our emotional intelligence brings to the scene—such as the need for reasonable working conditions, and safety—is a pure nuisance to industry. Modern technology is solving the nuisance problem by introducing *actual* robots, which eliminate the need for humans, altogether. So, as a result of more knowledge, our spirits end up even more separated, more unwanted, more unloved, and more unhappy, to which humans respond by seeking salvation through even more information. It's a cycle of increasing unhappiness that, should we remain trapped in it, will never end, *until the "house of cards" one day falls, and everything ends.*

In effect, humanity is trying to replace with mountains of accumulated knowledge the continuity of awareness that our innate wisdom naturally provides, when we are spiritually free. In doing so, we have unintentionally created a world in which our spirits are not wanted. This world sees no value in the wisdom of the human soul, the wisdom whose influence makes us feel and behave like humans. It values only the brain's ability to manipulate knowledge in pursuit of economic gain.

From the perspective of governments—justified, as they are, by this mountain of information—our spiritual needs are inconvenient and troublesome. People who believe in governments, and in the information that justifies them, are endlessly asking: "*Why can't people just obey all the rules?"* Wouldn't life, then, be like Heaven? The fact is, our lives are decidedly not like Heaven—even when we obey the rules.

Governed, as we are, by rules which force us to repress the messages emanating from our souls, it is impossible for us to perfectly comply. Thus, we see ourselves as imperfect. We then compound the injury by concluding that we must be evil, because we don't feel like obeying all the rules.

Indeed, our governments do see our spirits as evil. *"How dare we be true to romantic attraction,"* when doing so doesn't comply with the laws governing marriage! Holding us to a standard that requires us to renounce feelings of romance is the ultimate offence that institutions commit against the human race. Romance, after all, evolved to govern procreation, by determining when, and how often, procreation occurs. This is not a small thing, both elements being crucial to the wellbeing of our species.

Moral edicts are civilized man's attempt to "fool" with Mother Nature, by playing God. So, not only do our governments see our spirits as evil, from the perspective of the industrial world it's clear that our emotional needs are a nuisance. Little wonder unhappiness and anxiety are ever-increasing problems throughout the land.

Social media and smart phones—mankind's most recent "world changing" invention—are contributing to an epidemic of stress-related disorders and antisocial behavior. This happens because social media ignores a fundamental limitation of the human brain: The brain evolved to maintain social order within the context of an extended family, and a community of such families. Not only does ignoring this limitation of the brain result in anti-social behaviors, but proponents of social media insist that mass communications will unite the world, when in fact it divides the world. Here is how:

Civil cultures are ideologically based. Thus, for a state to exist, its subjects must be comprehensively indoctrinated in the ideology on which the culture is founded. But all ideologically based cultures force people to ignore their inborn sensibilities, to survive. To find relief from the emotional insult of spiritual repression, people employ social media to unload on each other with arguments based on conflicting beliefs, ideologies, propaganda, etc., each of which presume to solve the unsolvable problem of how to organize mankind en masse. By propagating divergent beliefs within cultures that require a unity of belief to even exist, social media will eventually render civil rule impossible, other than by tyranny—which would prohibit communication entirely, on pain of imprisonment or death.

If that's not enough, we moderns are on the precipice of another technological revolution that is the product of accumulated knowledge—artificial intelligence (AI). It is ironic that human intelligence—already off course, since the moment it outlawed its genetic wisdom—is about to unleash on the world a much more powerful intelligence that is without genetic wisdom, thus has no connection to life, whatsoever. Having ignored the wisdom of our souls, we are largely functioning as though we have no souls. As a consequence, we are blind to the implications of what we are doing. Now, with AI, we can do it all much faster.

Because of the remarkable technological progress that has occurred during the last few centuries, we have come to associate what it means to be human, largely, with being intelligent. From this perspective, many might conclude that AI is making us more human. I disagree. Evolutionary programming is what makes us human, not the brain's ability to manipulate and contemplate information.

Human brains are programmed to take care of the life of our species through interdependent relationships. That programming defines what it means to be human, not our intelligence. Whenever we do anything—other than serve life, in ways inspired by our evolutionary programming—we are not being human. We are instead functioning as robots programmed to serve the illusion that we are in control of life. That illusion results in mindlessness, as exemplified by a recent report about how China is employing AI.

> China is using artificial intelligence to build the ultimate surveillance state. Many of China's ubiquitous surveillance cameras feed into an A.I. system that recognizes faces, figures out your name, and alert authorities if you disobey the law. Even crossing the street, you are on camera. If you jaywalk, you'll be caught, shamed, and fined. Citizens will be ranked with a social credit score. That score will be affected even by the social credit scores of people you hang out with. If your score drops below a certain threshold, you will be denied access to places like train stations and airports. China is playing a long game, trying to dominate a technology that will allow it to monitor its population in unprecedented detail and become the 21st century superpower.
>
> —Richard Engle, The Today Show

Is this what we really want, a world in which power is associated with surveillance. Unless the human spirit regains control through sisterhoods and brotherhoods, that's what's coming. When serving the illusion on which civil rule stands—the idea that mankind is in control of life—the smarter we are, the more trouble we get ourselves into. Had evolution made humans less intelligent, maybe we wouldn't have invented the atomic bomb. What a blessing it would be if that weapon didn't exist.

I'm not suggesting that being less intelligent will save us. I'm saying we need to quit misusing the intelligence we have. Evolution gave us that intelligence, just as it did the wisdom that is seated in our souls. Yet we misuse our intelligence, every time we act on the illusion that we are somehow in control of life. Given that we have lost our way, the last thing we need is to bring online an even more powerful intelligence than the human brain's.

By posing a challenge to human intelligence, AI is forcing us to contemplate a crucial matter: What does it mean to be human? If it forces us to answer that question, AI may turn out to be mankind's greatest blessing. It will be the spur that calls to our attention the mistake we made 6000 years ago, when we outlawed the wisdom of our souls in the name of social order. It was no small mistake, for it transformed humans from celebrators of life to celebrators of illusions.

Human beings now live as if we have no souls. This explains our propensity to seek salvation in limitless growth—in information, technology, control, and accomplishments. Limitless growth is the definition of Cancer, an entity that can't stop growing. As with a Cancer, our need for ever-more-accomplishments *will* eventually end—either when we surrender our designs on the future and accept the guidance of our souls, or when unlimited growth destroys its host, our species.

Limitless growth will be cured once we recognize that the future is unknowable, therefore uncontrollable. Once that happens, we will immediately realize that our designs on the future are illusions, and start figuring out how to surrender them. As things stand, even if we recognize that the future can't be controlled, we have no choice but to act as if it could be. It's the only way to survive the circumstances imposed by institutional subjugation. So, for now, we remain frozen in our ongoing effort to accomplish a task that common sense tells us is not possible.

But let's be kind to ourselves, in the sense that Jesus was kind—indeed, he even forgave the soldiers who crucified him. Like those soldiers, we can't be blamed for what we must do, to survive, even if what we do makes no sense from a commonsense perspective—Christ's perspective.

Humanity has been suffering for thousands of years, since we stopped serving life. We are indeed starving for wisdom, but, not because we don't have it at hand. It is because we are paying no attention to the messages of innate wisdom—the pain and pleasure that let us know when we are, or are not, serving life. For modern humans, the messages of pain will never stop coming from our souls, until we heed them. But, given institutional subjugation, we must continue to ignore them, as surely as a trained animal must repress its inborn sensibilities, in order to make it in the human world.

As it has for all species, evolution endowed homo sapiens with all the wisdom necessary to take care of life. As the pain of ignoring our innate wisdom inexorably increases, it will spur us to find relief, by figuring out how to surrender our designs on the future. With no future to attend to, we will be free to take pleasure in the unbreakable bonds inherent to sisterly-brotherly love—the same pleasure the Pirahã people experience every day of their lives.

Taking care of life, when it happens, will be the unintended consequence of regaining our natural state of contentment, as surely as not taking care of life was the unintended consequence of trying to control the future, by force of law.

CHAPTER NINE

A Status Akin to Religion

How the Practice of Marriage led to Institutional Subjugation

It may be hard for modern people to believe this, but there was a time when humans lived without institutions, and their rules and laws. Even more incomprehensible to us is what it was like to live back then.

A quote by Olympic medal winner Chris Mazder gives us a glimpse of what life was like when it was governed by feelings, prior to the rise of institutions. He was describing how it felt to be the first American to win a medal in men's luge, but his words reveal how bereft is modern life of the mutual caring that is inherent to mankind's natural way of life.

> "All the energy is brought by the incredible fans who traveled here, family, friends. Like the entire US Luge Association was here, and you could feel that energy. But it's more than just energy. It's the fact that they are there for you, win or lose, and that gives you the confidence to just go for it 100%. It's just feeling the security."

What would it be like to feel that secure—to feel that everyone around us was totally there for us, win or lose? That sense of contentment and security is how primitive people felt all the time. When modern humans observe primitive people, we discount their existence as insignificant, compared to ours, because we judge their state of being in materialistic terms—the only sense of wellbeing we have ever known—and we are not impressed. We fail to realize that our primitive ancestors were immersed for their entire lives in the experience of *living* what Mazder merely glimpsed for a moment. They lived a way of life in which everyone around them was there for them 100%, win or lose.

But, feelings ceased to govern human life, when men claimed the right to own women, through the practice of marriage. At that point, our primitive ancestors ceased to be there for each other. With the advent of marriage, abstract values and prohibitions suddenly appeared, such as faithfulness, paternity, adultery, legitimacy. These concerns had devastating effects on the relationships of contentment, intimacy, and interdependence that had previously bonded the members of spiritual homes in spiritual trust.

In order to justify the idea that men had the right to own women, the institution of marriage had to be sanctified as having a higher purpose, a relationship between a man and a woman that would make the world a better place than it was when men and women related normally.

In essence, marriage constituted the first religion, immediately achieving a religiouslike status that is sustained to this day. Humans continue to believe in marriage, despite the fact that the arrangement consistently fails to fulfill its promises of stable human relationships, functionality, a viable place to raise children, and "happiness ever after."

Marriage may have been the first institution, but all the institutions that have followed fail us in the same two ways. They destroy the intimacy of sisterhood-brotherhood—the most essential legacy of evolution—and none of them can make good on what they promise. We are left to suffer the consequences. Though we suffer, we presently have no choice but to subjugate ourselves to their rule. Without interdependent relationships, the relationships that the institution of marriage destroyed, people have since been totally dependent on institutions, for survival.

Modern people tend to believe that civil rule came about because of the practice of agriculture. I argue that it actually began with the practice of marriage, when it was introduced into primitive cultures. Marriage, and all the institutions that followed, were the building blocks of the modern mass society that now emotionally imprisons mankind. The belief that underpinned marriage is the same one that now justifies all institutions—a belief that defies common sense. It's the belief that humans can control outcomes into the indefinite future, by force of manmade laws.

Ignored, however—amid our human passion to protect ourselves into the distant future—is the inconvenient fact that the future can't be controlled. Civil rule represents mankind's futile attempt to make the unknowable knowable. As powerful as it has become in governing the lives of all humankind, civilization is, in essence, nothing more than a patchwork of invented ideas, cultural practices, and preferred behaviors whose status has been sanctified by force of law. That law, standing on a parapet of belief alone, can only be described or understood as a form of religion.

Before men invented marriage, sisterhoods formed the core of every extended human family. Their spiritual authority was the source of order and purpose in human life, making it possible for humans to live in the intimacy and spiritual freedom of interdependence. The practice of males owning females destroyed the sisterhoods, and the spiritual authority through which females had always established and maintained a natural sense of order.

Until sisterhoods were destroyed, they reigned as the crucial moderating presence, among humans organically linking the members of primitive families in a circle of interdependence that can only be described as love. The elimination of sisterhoods destroyed natural social order among humans and left men with an identity crisis. Men's natural role, to support and protect the sisterhood and their children, evaporated. Suddenly, without sisterhoods, there was nothing for men to do, and no reference for order.

In the absence of sisterhoods, men faced two questions that previously had never existed: Why am I here? And how do we maintain order? To answer those questions, men invented religion, in their newfound belief that their purpose was to obey the universe's creator, God. If they did that, they presumed, there would be order. The aggrandizement of males, through religious practices—including projecting the image of God as a male—universally enhanced their social status, relative to females. In some primitive cultures, religiouslike practices reached the extremes of blood sacrifices, cannibalism, and headhunting—the unintended consequences of the original mistake men made, by granting themselves the right to own women.

Religiouslike practices separated our species from its natural matriarchal roots, by imposing the patriarchal—thus, hierarchical—systems that continue to rule us, today. The "cancerous blight" on the face of this planet which civil rule has become is the ultimate consequence of the destruction of sisterly bonds, through the practice of marriage. It is impossible to overstate either the elemental potency of the sisterly bonds, or the destructive effects the imposition of marriage inflicted on early cultures—and continues to inflict, to this day.

The influence of the sisterhoods was a powerful elemental force essential for order, and for mankind's ability to live in concert with the forces of Nature that created us. Unlike the simplistic, yet burdensome, system of moral absolutes introduced by marriage, the sisterhood's authority rested lightly on the free human spirits who followed its implicit dictates, without any sensation of compulsion or direction. Had the innate spiritual guidance of sisterhoods remained in force, institutional subjugation would neither have been needed, nor conceived. The sisterhoods would never have put up with it, nor would the women of today, if they were bonded in spiritual trust.

The centrality of the sisterhoods to human life dates from the very origins of our emotional heritage, as social primates. Our natural way of life, as members of a social species, fulfilled both our spiritual and material needs. To have contentment and happiness, as humans, we need to live in social groups bonded by love. The loss of the sisterhoods decimated those bonds, yet our organic need for them, which defines the very nature of the human spirit, has never changed. It lives on in modern women, who retain their evolutionary connection with their spirits. The loss of sisterhoods destroyed mankind's connection to life, and only when the women of today regain their spiritual authority, through sisterhood, will mankind's connection to life be restored.

That reconnection will occur when a group of women—any group of women who are close friends—fully recognize the depth of their soul-felt need for one another—a depth that goes to the level of emotional survival, itself. Yes, even in the midst of modern mass culture, natural social order can begin again. And it will be a profound experience for those involved, given the virtual nonexistence of unconditional love and spiritual honesty in our modern world.

Considering the degree to which modern humans are separated from any sense of natural order, it may seem like a pie-in-the-sky idea that it can be regained. Our souls are aware of the myriad signs of social disintegration and emotional suffering afflicting humanity, hence, the growing unease that is felt by all. Thus, few of us remain unaware that something we don't understand is going on, and that it is terribly wrong. Indeed, few humans alive, today, would fail to admit that they are poignantly aware of a soul-felt hunger for unconditional love—and for spiritual freedom, though they don't necessarily use that specific term.

The fact that all modern humans still feel such a strong need for these things, after thousands of years living under the complete domination of manmade institutions, is a testament to the indelible nature of our connection to our evolutionary—our natural—roots. Unconditional love is essential for human happiness. Full stop. And the enduring desire for spiritual freedom, among modern humans, demonstrates the universality of that desire in all members of our species. It is such a natural thing—our yearning for the freedom to simply do what we feel like doing in the light of our immediate circumstances. It is a freedom that the members of *no* other species have ever stopped enjoying. We continue to feel this need, despite the fact that our physical survival in a civilized world depends on strict obedience to all the rules and laws that define that world.

Though we long for these freedoms, it's a fact that billions of human spirits perpetually suffer the consequences of living in a world which outlaws spiritual honesty, thus relegates unconditional love to the category of foolish thoughts. If truth be told, the frustration and despair, the headaches and acid reflux, and the uncountable other negatives we consciously endure, are testaments to the fact that our spirits struggle to contain their recurring impulses to throw off the emotional enslavement that has resulted from humanity's fatal act of folly in abandoning sisterhoods.

As a consequence of that struggle, our trust in institutions as the regulators of our lives is a troubled one. We are painfully aware that institutions are unworthy of that trust. Yet, we keep trusting them—not because we really believe in them, or because of their religiouslike status, but by default. In the absence of sisterhoods, we have no other way to survive, and nothing else to depend on for order. Sisterhoods, after all, are the unifying core of the natural human family. They were the cradles in which Homo Sapiens developed and thrived, and the source of order throughout evolution.

CHAPTER TEN

Why Soldiers Find it Difficult to Come Home from War

Mazder's account, in the previous chapter, about how he felt on becoming the first American to win an Olympic medal in men's luge, underscores a crucial truth: We modern humans have never lost the emotional ability to experience unconditional love—the state of being in which pre-humans, then humans thrived, throughout evolution. However, we experience unconditional love only rarely, and in small doses—as, in the wake of natural disasters, or among soldiers who face, together, the dangers of war. Indeed, the sensation of unconditional love is so rarely experienced, among civilized humans, that the phenomenon is viewed as an aberration of reality. "People may have experienced it in war, or when helping each other in disaster situations, but those situations are not normal. Out here in the 'real' world, unconditional love doesn't happen."

The world that's real to the civilized mind, it turns out, is unreal to the human spirit. The only world the human spirit recognizes as real is the one that existed before the advent of institutions, when people survived by depending on each other. The human spirit comes alive in relationships of interdependence, as evidenced by what soldiers experience on the field of battle.

In his Ted Talk, entitled "Why Veterans Miss War," wartime correspondent Sebastian Junger describes how profoundly soldiers are affected by the intimacy of wartime experiences. Through their interdependent relationships, as soldiers, men experience the feelings inherent to a spiritual home. In the interests of brevity, I largely paraphrase Junger's remarks, below, while retaining the first-person style of his narrative:

> At Restrepo—a military outpost in Afghanistan—every guy up there was almost killed, including me and my good friend Tim Hetherington, who was later killed in Libya. The boys are up there for a year. I was particularly close to a guy named Brendan O'Byrne. When he came back, I invited him to a dinner party. He was talking to one of my friends, who knew how bad it had been out there. She asked him, "Is there anything at all that you miss about the war?" After thinking about it for quite a while, he finally said, "Ma'am, I miss almost all of it." And he's one of the most traumatized people I've seen from that war.
>
> What was he talking about when he said he misses the war? He's not a psychopath. He doesn't miss killing people. He's not crazy. He doesn't miss getting shot at. He doesn't miss seeing his friends getting killed. What is it that he misses? I think what he misses is brotherhood.
>
> He misses, in some ways, the opposite of killing. What he misses is connection to the other men. Brotherhood is different from friendship. Friendship happens in society. The more you like someone, the more you would be willing to do for them. Brotherhood has nothing to do with how you feel about the other person. It's an [implicit] mutual agreement that each will put the

safety of all other members of the group above his own. In effect, you are saying "I love these other people more than I love myself."

Brenden was the leader of a four-man team, and his worst day wasn't when he was almost killed. The worst thing that happened was when he thought one of his men had been killed—later to discover that he had been knocked unconscious by a bullet that had struck his helmet. Afterward, he realized that he could not protect his men, and that was the only time Brenden cried in Afghanistan. That's brotherhood! In WWII, there were many stories about men who slipped out of the windows or doors of field hospitals, still wounded, so they could rejoin their brothers out there.

You think about these soldiers having an experience like that—a bond like that, in a small group where they loved 20 other people more than they loved themselves. Think about how good that feels. Imagine it. Imagine these men being blessed with that experience for a year or so, and then they come home and are thrust back into the impersonal atmosphere that the rest of us are used to, where nobody knows who they can really count on, who loves them, whom they can love, or what anyone would do for them, if it came down to it. That is terrifying. Psychologically, war is easy, compared to that kind of alienation. That's why soldiers miss combat.

As can be seen from that narrative, brotherhood happens—indeed, it's unavoidable when a group of people are dependent on one another for survival. Brotherhood reconnects people with their innate wisdom, through which they discover that it is their very nature to be more concerned about the group's wellbeing, than their own. The experience of loving the people around us more than we love ourselves is not rational or intentional, nor can it be learned or taught. It's hard-wired, because our species' survival has depended on it, throughout evolution.

Indeed, through interdependent relationships, soldiers experience the unconditional love that is inherent to natural human relationships. But, since success in the institutionalized world requires independence, not interdependence, we moderns view the unconditional love those soldiers experienced as an aberration of reality, using terms such as "trauma bonding" to explain it.

Returning soldiers come from a world in which they experienced a profound sense of caring and being cared for. They come back to a world where brotherhood does not exist. Spousal relationships seldom fill the need. This is not the fault of the spouse, but of the nature of the relationship. (Social primates are social bonders by instinct, not pair-bonders, and do not form lifetime bonds with one other individual, male or female.) So, returning vets have no natural sense that their lives are of value to anyone. That's disconcerting, depressing, and terrifying.

In another Ted Talk entitled, "Our Lonely Society Makes It Hard to Come Home from War," Junger makes another observation that further sheds spiritual light on our circumstances. I paraphrase again:

In every war America has fought, including the Civil War, the intensity of the fighting has decreased, in terms of casualty rates. But, the mental disability rates have gone up. In Iraq and Afghanistan, the casualty rate was one third what it was in Vietnam, but the disability rate was three times higher. These numbers seemed wrong.

Having a background in anthropology, Junger spent considerable time studying why the disability rates did not correlate with the intensity of the fighting. He concluded that what happens in combat isn't the problem.

The problem, Junger continued, is the ever-increasing alienation our soldiers face, when they come home. Our country is now so divided that the two political parties are literally accusing each other of treason, of trying to undermine the security and the welfare of their own country. The gap between rich and poor keeps growing. Race relations are getting worse. Veterans know that any tribe—or any platoon—that treated itself that way would never survive. But our society has gotten used to it. Veterans have gone away and are coming back and seeing their own country with fresh eyes. They see what's going on. This is the country they fought for. No wonder they're depressed. No wonder they're scared. Sometimes we ask ourselves if we can save the vets. I think the real question is: Can we save ourselves?

To save ourselves, we need to rediscover the brotherhood we're hardwired for—the same brotherhood that those young men experienced at war. But, brotherly love does not result from intent; circumstances make it happen. The young soldiers Junger talks about did not go to war with the intent of experiencing brotherhood. Like us, they had no idea that such an experience even existed.

Brotherhood *happened to them!* The circumstances of combat graced their lives with a situation that caused it to happen. Suddenly, their sense of wellbeing was more dependent on the wellbeing of their fellow soldiers, than on the "wellbeing" of their legal and monetary identities. Indeed, in Restrepo, their legal and economic status had no significance at all, which is why they were free to live in the moment— *the only circumstance in which brotherhood can exist.*

Based on the experience of those soldiers, it becomes apparent what stands between us and sisterhood and brotherhood. It's our monetary and legal identities, which civilized people must spend their entire lives protecting. But, when everything has a price on it—including the services provided by humans—and every livable parcel of land is under the jurisdiction of a legal system, how can anyone survive on this planet without a monetary and legal identity? No one can. We moderns have no choice but to accept the rule of money and law, and the identity that goes with it, for the sake of our physical survival. As a result, sisterhood and brotherhood do not exist in our world. Consequently, we are not all that happy.

The long and short of it is that to live on Planet Earth these days requires a "permit"—a monetary and legal identity. To qualify, we must obey every law and assume total responsibility for our personal wellbeing. This is the opposite of what Nature requires of us to live on earth— that we be true to the wisdom of our souls, through which we assume absolute responsibility for the wellbeing of our sisters and brothers. We are "spiritually wired" to satisfy Nature's requirements, not the state's. That's why brotherhood is so remarkable and spontaneous an experience, whenever the circumstances of interdependence exist.

As members of a social species, we can't physically survive the natural world, alone. This makes humans dependent beings, by our very nature. Every human, therefore, is dependent, for survival, on either a legal and monetary identity—as in modern life—or a family consisting of a sisterhood and brotherhood—as was the case throughout evolution. Our legal and monetary identities give us powers to do things that spiritually free people could not imagine. But when we recognize the spiritual price we pay for that power, which is a life without intimacy, we might be inspired to reconsider our need for the relationships of sisterhood and brotherhood, in which our souls are our guides. Then we, too, will experience the same unconditional love that those soldiers knew in Restrepo.

CHAPTER ELEVEN

Our Two Selves

At a family gathering shortly before his death, President George H. W. Bush was asked what advice he would have for his great granddaughter, based on what he had learned throughout his long and storied life. After gazing upon the infant for a moment, he replied, "To thine own self be true." That Shakespearian phrase is often quoted—perhaps because people put so much hope in it. People seem to universally feel that life would be in capable hands, if we were all true to our authentic selves. But, as subjects of institutions, we survive by complying with manmade laws, which leave none of us free to be true to our real selves. This book is my effort to convince people that life *will* again be in qualified hands, when humans can once-again be true to our innately based feelings—after thousands of years of institutional subjugation.

Before the existence of tribal, then, civil authorities, people had only one "self"—the "real" one we are born with. As exemplified by the Pirahã people, who still live without laws, marriage, or governments, humans are entirely capable of living happy, reasonable, orderly and self-respecting lives, when being true to their real selves. But there came a time in human history when humans began trying to control the future, through culturally imposed mores and laws. That resulted in the universal appearance of a second self—an "indoctrinated" self whose behavior is controlled by the institutions that rule our lives. Being possessed by two selves, humans have existed in a state of self-conflict, ever since.

Each self has its own perspective on life, and the differences could not be greater. The indoctrinated self's sensibilities are based on legally imposed laws that inform us of how to personally survive our future. It lives for the future, thus, is dependent on the "tools" provided by monetary and legal systems to even exist.

The real self, on the other hand, lives in the moment. Its sensibilities are based on genetically endowed wisdom which informs us about how to serve life in our relationships with the people around us. It places no value in the future promised by *anything*, much less law and money. It doesn't even recognize that institutions exist. Because the real self doesn't recognize that institutions exist, there is no place for who we really are in the institutionalized world.

Only indoctrinated selves have a place in the modern world. So, when someone tells us, "to thine own self be true," we eagerly agree, because, above all else, that is what our souls desire. But, as institutional subjects, we agree in vain, because we are accountable to the law for the sake of our very survival. As a result, we are true to our indoctrinated selves, whether we realize it or not.

And there are consequences for that. For thousands of years, our species' life has not been in capable hands. *Our indoctrinated selves accept, as real, only what is required for us to physically survive the institutionalized reality in which we live, where each individual is responsible for his own future.* Our real selves, our capable ones, who live exclusively in the moment, know infinitely more about life than our indoctrinated ones. But we pay no attention to what our souls know, even though great playwrights, artists, composers and storytellers are constantly informing us of what we really know. We have no choice but to conduct our day-to-day lives as if we don't know what the artists are telling us, for the sake of our material survival in the modern world.

Another consequence of having to be true to our indoctrinated selves is that we must make many major decisions throughout our lives that we would prefer not to have to make, regarding careers, jobs, purchases, and relationships. Whenever we find that we are talking ourselves into a decision, it signals that there is a struggle going on between our two selves. Be forewarned that, the more you rationalize, in these situations, to convince yourself that you are making the right choice, the more likely you are to suffer from the decision. The amount of self-convincing you need is a measure of the spiritual dishonesty required to arrive at the decision. If spiritually free to live in the moment, decisions that affect your future for life, and the rationalizations required to make them, are not necessary. People simply react to the moment in accordance with their innate wisdom—their map of life—and life goes on.

> *There is a truth in the music. Too bad that we, as a culture, have not been able to address that truth. That's the shame of it. Not letting that truth be our truth.*
>
> —Wynton Marsalis in Ken Burn's documentary, "Country Music."

There is an enormous tension between our two selves—one who lives in the moment, the other only for the future. In modern life, where everyone must live for the future, the indoctrinated self has the upper hand—to such an extent that neither we, nor our legal systems, recognize that we have a real self. Though our real self is repressed to the point of nonexistence, it remains the expression of the genetic code that defines what it means to be human. So, the immense tension continues to exist.

I believe the tension between our two selves is the primary source of neurosis in modern man. Emotional disorders are the organisms' only possible response to living a life loaded with contradictions.

Since our indoctrinated selves don't recognize the existence of our real ones, or even comprehend *why* they exist, there is currently no path to resolution. We are stuck with the resulting emotional suffering whose vastness was made evident in 2019, when Oprah announced her partnership with Prince Harry, of England, for the production of a new series on mental health:

> "Our new, but yet-unnamed, multi-part series focuses on mental health and how the scourge of depression and anxiety, post-traumatic stress disorder, addiction, trauma and loss, is devastating lives daily across the globe."

I am grateful to Oprah and Prince Harry for bringing attention to this suffering, and trust that their desire to bring change will help many people. My ultimate concern, however, is that not much can be done, from within the context of modern life. To regain our mental health, we must trust our souls, not our plans, if we are ever to have the needs of only the real self, to satisfy. That's a tall order, for it requires that we divorce ourselves from the promise of institutions, thus from the only identity and sense of wellbeing we have ever known.

Though our indoctrinated selves don't recognize the existence of our real ones, they *do* sense that something within us tirelessly seeks to foil their plans. They don't realize that what they are sensing is the real self's desire to take care of life. Our real selves place no value in the things that define the indoctrinated way of life—money, property, legally obligated relationships, plans, beliefs, dreams… These values are destroyers of life, not its caretakers. Indeed, on occasion, our real selves inspire us to do things that flagrantly defy those values. It's understandable, therefore, that the indoctrinated world perceives the real human self as the seat of evil, the source of sin, disorder, and social upheaval—a view that is prevalent among the world's great religions who proclaim that humans are born in sin.

Humans are hard-wired to experience happiness and contentment when the needs of our real selves, our animal selves, are satisfied. Given that fact, is it any wonder that the issues to which Oprah referred are so problematic in modern life? Human contentment requires spiritual freedom, a way of life in which the world becomes a playground for the soul. The real self takes pleasure in the intimacy of interdependent relationships, while the indoctrinated self feeds on objectives to be won. For the indoctrinated self, life is not a playground. It's a workshop—a place where humans work at being better people, and toil at realizing plans, objectives, and dreams.

The institutional indoctrination of modern humanity has transformed human behavior from natural to unnatural. The natural humans who once reaped all the spiritual wealth life has to offer, through taking care of the needs of those around them, now eke out survival from the "Monopoly" game that life has become. In the modern paradigm, we have become scheming, self-serving characters who spend our entire lives focused on "winning" the only game we are allowed to play. In a world in which our only means of survival is to accumulate wealth and property, our souls recoil from the greed and scheming tactics of our indoctrinated selves. In such an atmosphere, humans tend to avoid meaningful relationships, altogether.

At times, we find it hard even to live with ourselves, because messages of guilt, contrition and shame continue to issue from our souls, reminding us that our behavior is falling short of Nature's standard. But we're not getting the message. Though we know something is wrong, we don't know what it is, or what to do about it. Some seek redemption through good deeds, or sacrifices, such as going to war to defend institutions. Others find whatever relief they can in prayer, through which people seek the favors and/or forgiveness of "their creator."

There is no other choice, because our modern world banishes from our lives the only real salvation—the unconditional love inherent to the interdependent relationships that all homo sapiens once knew. It is the same unconditional love that our soldiers experienced on the battlefield in Afghanistan. As true believers in our modern paradigm, those soldiers went to war to be true to their indoctrinated selves. They were possessed with the same illusion that afflicts all modern people—the conviction that we *know how things should be*. Indeed, they were so certain of their "truth" that they were willing to place their lives on the line, to make things right, as defined by the ideology to which they were subject.

But, upon arrival at that remote military outpost, they found themselves entirely dependent on one another for survival. In that instant—that's all it takes!—their indoctrinated selves ceased to exist, and their real selves appeared. Suddenly, they were no longer governed by the virtue of their cause, but by their innate sense of need and concern for one another. Spiritual freedom transformed that military outpost from a place of danger, fear, and dread, to a playground for their souls. It was a phenomenon that not one of them had experienced in their entire lives. In "Restrepo"—the documentary about these soldiers—the outpost was referred to as a "man Eden." They hadn't found salvation in good works and righteousness, as they had expected. They found it in brotherhood, the only place where salvation for the human soul exists.

Twice in my life, for three or four days at a time, I have been in situations where I have experienced the same sensation of unconditional love for others that I believe those soldiers did. During my experiences, my beliefs vanished, too, and my designs on the future along with them. These were transformative experiences. Having spent my entire life living for the future, burdened with the need to pursue lifetime objectives, it was suddenly as if the future and its burdens didn't exist. During those experiences of living in the moment, I felt as-one with the people around me, and with life.

These experiences were so remarkable and comforting that they are, in large part, the reason my thesis on spiritual freedom exists. My concern is this: How was it possible for me to experience the unconditional love that I shared during those encounters—one planned, the other quite by happenstance? They were, after all, experiences with which I was totally unfamiliar.

If it's possible for humans to experience this kind of intimacy, doesn't that mean we were born to experience it? If so, then why aren't we experiencing it through our entire lives? I asked myself this question: The answer, I have come to believe, is: Yes, that is exactly how we are meant to live! In this book, I investigate that possibility and share my sense of what happened to cause humans to accept a way of life that is the exact opposite, one in which we live for the future in a state of spiritual estrangement.

Within the compartmentalized world perceived by our indoctrinated minds, we humans live under the presumption that we have free will. We believe we are the authors of our own ideas, and that our behaviors are expressions of those ideas. We believe that human possibilities are limited only by our imaginations. On the other hand, life is very different for our real selves, for whom the miracle of life unfolds without intent, as the real self bears witness to it. Its responses and behaviors are expressions of the instincts that communicate, via feelings, the optimal response to whatever situation is at hand. The real self is directly connected to life by the unconditional love and contentment it experiences through interdependent human relationships. In that state of ultimate emotional resolution, life feels complete, and the very idea of limitless possibilities becomes meaningless.

Our indoctrinated selves indulge themselves in the belief that humanity has broken free of the chains of Nature, by virtue of the power of our own imaginations. Institutions teach us that, with their help, we humans can lift ourselves, by our own bootstraps, from a world of insignificance to one of grandeur. This is the rationale that fuels mankind's illusion that we have dominion over the forces of Nature that created us, and that, in effect, we are like gods. But, no matter how materially grand our hoped-for future might turn out to be, the future of anyone possessed with the "god delusion" will be a future without love.

The god delusion is not something people take on intentionally, or by free will. It's the unintended consequence of civilized man's independent way of life. Given that monetary and legal systems render each person exclusively responsible for his own wellbeing, we have no choice, other than to presume that we are in control of our destiny—the presumption upon which the god delusion stands.

Recovery from the God delusion is something that no human can manage, alone. We were not born to control life—neither ours nor anyone else's. We were born to participate in life. But, life only happens in a spiritual home, a place where people live in the moment, and in a state of intimacy—the only home our real selves have ever known.

CHAPTER TWELVE

A Spiritual Home

Spiritual Trust, the Foundation of a Spiritual Home

The human soul has an absolute need for relationships of spiritual trust. It is non-negotiable. It is a key element of a way of life eons in the making. Like the absolute need in the hearts of all tigers, to live solitary lives, our innate human need for relationships of spiritual trust is a product of billions of minute, incremental changes that took place over an incomprehensibly long passage of time. Every detail of the way of life of every species has this same weight of meaning, a meaning that goes far beyond the mere concept of variation.

When we look upon a living human, or an animal—even a tick, or an individual microbe—we are witnesses to a masterpiece of serendipity, not design. For, each change is a roll of the dice, the guessing of a number between one and one billion—an impossible win, when it comes out improving the life of a species—the very heart of the definition of serendipity. This is the miracle of evolution, which pre-writes the general direction of the story of any living being, creating the parameters within which all choices will be made, spelling out the options best applied—all to prepare each individual organism to respond promptly, and most efficaciously, to the changes taking place in an unpredictable natural world.

The background awareness, in all humans, of the everpresence of potential danger, is the trigger that ignited, and still ignites, the *felt need* of each individual to bond with others. Evolution didn't provide us with claws, fangs, and thick fur, so our primitive ancestors naturally had to gravitate together in spiritual trust, by surrendering to the absolute truth about humans—that we are not tigers, thus, cannot survive the natural world, alone. So, it's quite possibly the most telling feature of our identity, as homo sapiens, that we absolutely need each other. A gravitas and sense of safety take form, when humans merge into a larger, more protective unit that is capable of defeating dangers that no individual could survive, alone. It makes a powerful difference. But, this merging would not happen, among any specific group of people, were the deep desire to do it not already imprinted in our human souls. This is one of the myriad ways that evolutionary wisdom steers the lives of all animate beings.

In the modern world where humans now live, however, we experience only remnants of this innate desire to bond with, and help, each other—most notably, in crisis situations. It's the reason total strangers are so willing to place themselves in real danger—sometimes dying, in the process—to help another human being who is being attacked, is trapped in a burning car, or is stranded or hurt, in a disaster. Our heartfelt need for one another also explains why women love coffee klatches, and why men like to watch football games, together, in garages they call "man caves." We see it, too, in generous giving to charities, and in the universal felt need to have friends. Though, at best, these are caricatures of the far deeper spiritual trust and connection that primitive humans enjoyed, it's important to realize that they are *real responses* to the voice of the human spirit: Though it's been all-but-silenced by modern civilization, it has never stopped communicating, through our feelings, in this and other ways.

It is one of the ironies of modern institutional life that we can still respond, emotionally, to this need to be close to one another. But, when it comes to unnatural things, like property and money, we don't see ourselves as needing one another. We consider every person to be totally responsible for their own wellbeing.

Meanwhile, all animals, even the domesticated ones who live with us, still live life as they always have—in the moment, and in continuous connection with their spirits. It all goes on without their knowing it, for it is the way of things, in Nature, to operate seamlessly, and unbidden. Animals are spiritually free. They do whatever they feel like doing, at the time. Thus, their responses to each other, and to us, are always genuine. Whether it's jealousy, gratitude, excitement at greeting, or attack, we know exactly where they stand, because they have never stopped basing their relationships on spiritual trust.

Civilization can handle that, in animals, but never where people are concerned. Civilization has an absolute need for a prescribed social order. To maintain that order, it needs human behavior to be predictable. To ensure predictability, institutions have created a complex framework of rules, laws, contracts, and social mores. Whether intended, or unintended, this restrictive behemoth has harmed humanity, by cutting us off from the most poignant elements of our own human nature. Even though the feelings that once drove us are still there, still speaking to us, their messages are as muted, today, as our all-but-forgotten ability to bond in spiritual trust with those close to us. Under the continuous persuasion of the institutions that organize our lives, every human being—for thousands of years, now—has been taught from babyhood to repress the need for spiritual trust, and other natural impulses, in order to measure up to the rules, be respectable, and fit in. It's the only way to survive in a world which elevates "manmade" over "nature-made," and power and money over spiritual authority and sisterly or brotherly love. Our most omnipresent conscious urge, growing up in this paradigm, is the one that tells us, repeatedly, not to "rock the boat."

So much of our world doesn't feel right! And that message is still coming through. Yet, somehow, we are unaware—though not blissfully—of the cost of obeying manmade legal obligations, instead of our natural, spiritual ones. We're unaware of the cost, because of our own self-enforced repression of the innate feelings through which the wisdom of the human spirit would normally flow. Actually, it's multiple costs, with the one we consciously recognize being the generalized unhappiness that modern humans can't ignore—and also can't defeat, no matter how many self-help books we buy. Humanity, in general, is so unaware of what ails us that none of those self-help books has yet arrived at the core answer, which is that sadness, depression, anxiety, tiredness, and disaffection with our daily lives are direct consequences of the emotional isolation, and emotional limitations, placed on each of us by the modern way of life.

There is a good reason why we try to ignore these serious symptoms. We simply can't imagine questioning the nature of the society into which we were born. We think our discomfort is our own fault, and that there is no cure. "That's life," we say, meaning that it's just the bothersome side effects of life, itself (as if it were a natural thing). But, in truth, what we think of as real life is actually an artificial life humanity has inflicted on itself. And the inexplicable, intransigent emotional pain and anxiety we feel is an early sign of more to come. The pain we're feeling, today, in-fact presages the eventual demise of our species. Hence, this book, which has been written to suggest how to start on a path that will return us to our real homes.

Our starting point is the utter quandary in which we modern humans find ourselves. The invention of civilization, thousands of years ago, separated us from our human spirits, and from Nature. It imprisoned our lives in an artificial paradigm utterly foreign to our nature. That artificial paradigm forces us to live lives acting out behaviors that make us unhappy, because they do not come naturally to our spirits. Thus, it shuts us off from the defining element in our nature—our emotions, our human spirits—the source of all our needs and desires, which we were born to follow, but cannot follow, now. The life we lead requires spiritual repression to survive it, and it is killing our spirits, and will eventually kill our species.

What do we do about our predicament? That's a premature question, for, before we can do anything, we must recognize something— that Nature made us as we are. Institutions didn't make us. Nature gave us a human spirit whose sensibilities are unchangeable, because they are grounded in the wisdom of our souls. Civil rule, which is founded on the belief that mankind is in control, simply won't let us see that. Civilized people steadfastly believe that, with the proper education, environment, and instructions, we can live any way of life, and be content. Civilization's antidotes to unhappiness are simply more indoctrination, via education, therapy, or counseling.

The reason I believe there is a way out of our predicament is that all of civilization's controls are for naught. Either humans will recognize what's happened and recover our natural way of life, or humanity will cease to exist. Civilization can never expunge or change the nature of the human spirit. It is immutable. Our human spirit is pre-programmed by Nature as a permanent record of our evolutionary wisdom. So, it's from evolution that flow all the feelings motivating our desires and actions. Civilization doesn't know or care about this. It doesn't recognize that we were born to serve the species. Nor does it acknowledge that we have instincts—or that they are immutable. It expects us to devote ourselves to being whatever civilization wants us to be, and it sees any failure to find happiness in doing so as signifying that we're not well-intended enough, or trying hard enough. Civilization doesn't care that we'd have to change who we are, to find contentment in a way of life that's not natural.

Think of it this way. You can't train just any dog to herd sheep. Even if you could, it would never love herding sheep. Good sheep dogs are bred for it, the result of many successive matings of individuals possessed of a natural propensity for herding sheep. Such dogs love herding sheep, so, they virtually train themselves. In the same way, humans have been honed by evolution through countless successive matings of individuals who have a natural propensity for taking care of life. If we were spiritually free, we would be excellent at taking care of life with little or no training, and would love every minute of it. But civilization has created a world in which we must accumulate personal wealth, to survive. We've all been trained to be exclusively responsible for our own wellbeing. But, we can't be trained to love it. As beings who evolved to find contentment in taking care of life through serving each other, it is stressful for us to live by serving self, and this probably accounts for the alarming increase in stress-related disorders that is sweeping the country.

As subjugated people, we *have* tried to change who we are, in order to fit in—but to no avail. We must stop doing that. Not only is it making us unhappy, it keeps us on a trajectory that endangers the survival of our species. We need to reconnect with the kind of home in which all members of our species thrived—thrived, that is, until the day civilization was invented. To reconnect, we need, first, to fully understand that our innate needs cannot be changed by decree, nor can our human spirits. This knowledge must be brought to the conscious minds of all modern humans, if we are ever to free ourselves from institutional subjugation. Until we understand that our inborn sensibilities are not malleable, we will have no choice but to keep trying to change ourselves.

This cannot be stressed enough: *Our spirits define what it means to be human.* Only when we see that will we stop trying to solve our problems, by changing who we are. Only then will we seek relationships that satisfy the immutable needs of our spirits.

I fully realize what I'm asking, here. I'm asking modern humans to literally turn away from the only way of life we know. It is a dramatic shift in perspective. I know, because I've lived it. I have been asked how my own civilized mind became aware of the unchangeable quality of the human spirit, when no one else seems to have any sense of it, at all.

For me, it was the result of a unique combination of circumstances. I lived the first 43 years of my life with a brain rendered dysfunctional by severe Attention Deficit Disorder. I was able to materially survive institutional subjugation, supporting my family as an electronics engineer, but, I was incapable of emotionally adapting to it. When the condition was diagnosed, and effectively treated, my brain started functioning normally. But, having never really adapted to institutional subjugation, I had concerns that needed answering—things that don't bother people who are better adapted. I sensed that something was fundamentally wrong about human existence, something deeply hidden that was never going to be corrected by people trying to be better. But I had no idea what it was.

The other unusual aspect of my situation was that, as an electronics engineer, I was well versed in system control theory—the theory used to design controllers for missile guidance, cruise controls, etc. I decided to employ system control theory in my effort to understand why human life seems so out of control. As a result of that decision, I eventually made two unique observations regarding the human condition, which I explain below.

The cruise control of an automobile provides an excellent example of how a controller works. It fulfills its objective—to maintain a constant velocity—by automatically changing the throttle setting, as the car climbs and descends hills. The significance of system control theory becomes evident when you realize that a cruise control would not be needed, if there were no future uncertainties, such as hills. The throttle could simply be set to maintain a specific velocity. But, like a car on a hilly road, the life of a species faces all kinds of future uncertainties. It clearly needs a controller.

The human brain, I reasoned, must be the species' controller, and its objective must be to sustain the life of the species. (*What other objective could there possibly be?*) Instead of encountering hills, the brain encounters situations that result in emotions like anger, empathy, or feelings of romance. Through these feelings, and countless others, the conscious mind is made aware of the need to respond to the "hills" of life. In the natural world—before civilization—animate life on earth continued for hundreds of millions of years under the exclusive control of instincts. Feelings programmed by evolution inspired the behaviors required for each species to flourish.

Then, civilization came along, founded on the belief that the uncertainties of the future can be eliminated by force of manmade laws. *That belief changed everything.* From childhood, civilized humans are sternly taught that, if everyone obeys the laws, the road ahead will be smooth—no "hills" to react to. From this perspective, there is no need for instincts, no need for feelings, no need for a controller. We reveal our absolute trust in laws when we accept their promise, as embodied in the statement: "Get married and live happily ever after."

But what is a woman to do, who seeks contentment in the promise of marriage, when, down the road a bit, she finds that she is not happy? If she has a natural support system, a sisterhood, she will immediately do what her feelings are telling her to do, and leave the situation. In other words, she will react to the "hill" when she encounters it, because her innately based feelings will be in control. But, with no viable support system, and having invested her hopes for a home and family in the promise of marriage, she will hang in there, trying her hardest to make things right—sometimes at the cost of her life.

But, hanging in there, she's not being true to her feelings of the moment. Without the natural support of a sisterhood, she's not free to follow the guidance of her spirit. She has no choice, other than to surrender her life to the dictates of the law. By remaining in her dysfunctional relationship, this woman will sentence herself to the pain of spiritual repression, for life, in order to have a home and family, within a civil culture.

When I recognized that the only way to survive, or to have a family, in the modern institutional paradigm is to comply with the law, I arrived at my first unique observation on the human condition. I understood that *our species is no longer under the control of our innate wisdom,* which evolved for the singular purpose of assuring our species' survival.

If the last point I made, above, has caused you to think that we modern people are now responsible for saving the species, rest assured that no individual is capable of doing that. Saving the species is the objective of life, itself. Life pre-programmed our brains to want to do all the things that serve life. Our objective, as individuals, is to honor the wisdom that Nature has given us—the wisdom of our souls. We do this by simply being true to our feelings of the moment. *All life will ever ask of anyone is that we be true to ourselves. It's all any of us can ever do, on behalf of our own happiness, and our species' wellbeing.*

Only in a spiritual home can humans be true to themselves. We're made to bond in spiritual trust, in the context of sisterhoods and brotherhoods—our natural human support system. Even then, as members of a home in which we are accepted for who we are, nothing we do as individuals can save our species. That would require a significant portion of all the people on earth to regain their spiritual freedom. And, of course, it may never happen. But even if it doesn't, it's not our business to concern ourselves with whatever the rest of the human race is doing. Our only viable concern is to attend to the needs of the people we love. Once we understand the need to be true to the wisdom of our souls, we will realize that our only legitimate concerns are about people with whom we are emotionally connected, in the context of interdependent relationships.

I've been stressing the fact that the conscious mind is not aware of life's objective, because it doesn't need to know. Its actions are reactions to feelings. I want to add that the subconscious mind, which produces those feelings, is also unaware of life's objective—species survival. All the subconscious knows, or needs to know, is what genetic wisdom tells it. This is our evolutionary map of life, a built-in record of the best possible reaction to the situation at hand. With that information, the subconscious mind prepares the individual to react, by changing the body's chemical state. In other words, love, fear, anger, romance, fatigue, and hunger are feelings created by specific cocktails of chemicals that flood the body. The conscious mind recognizes the body's chemical state as a feeling. Then, it takes pleasure in instigating the activities required to return the body to its normal chemical state, by eating when hungry, serving the people we love, finding safety when afraid, and a place to rest when tired, etc. The ultimate and unavoidable consequence of animate beings satisfying their feelings of the moment is that life flourishes on this planet—a fact to which each of us owes our existence.

Thanks to the species' controller—the brain—all of this occurs automatically, without any entity on earth knowing that life's purpose is to ensure the survival of the species. It's the ultimate example of *the whole being much greater than the sum of the parts: The whole is able to fulfill life's objective, when there is no part of the whole that has any idea what that objective is.*

The second unique observation I gained from applying system control theory to life was that the *real organism is the species—not its individual members.* Thus, for a species to flourish, evolution must program the brain of each member to produce behavior that places the needs of the species above the individual's. But, things don't work that way, in the civilized world. Our purpose, as dependents of institutions, is to maintain civil order, thus, hold the needs of institutions sacrosanct, above the needs of any individual. This is why civilized people willingly surrender their lives, in times of war, so that their institutions can "live."

In the act of placing the needs of the state above our own, we moderns are unknowingly placing the state's needs above our species' needs. We have noted that, in the natural world, the brain's objective is the survival of the species. But, as a result of the indoctrination required to function in the civilized world, the modern brain's objective is the survival of the state. States promise us a certain, just, and safe future, a promise no state has ever fulfilled. Yet, via that promise, states have successfully hijacked our brains.

As a result, we moderns go about behaving as though our state is a "living organism" whose needs must be served, above all else, while we ignore the needs of life's real organism, our species. We see the state as the master of life, when, in fact, it has nothing to do with life, at all. It has no feelings, no soul. It demands only our compliance. It cares about nothing, not even its own existence, much less ours. The only reason we care that the state exists is that, having abandoned the support provided by natural human families, our survival totally depends on the social-legal structures provided by the state.

I believe the day will come when we surrender that dependence, by bonding in the interdependent relationships inherent to spiritual homes. When this occurs, states will evaporate like clouds in the sky, and not a soul will mourn their passing.

After I understood how modern human life defies natural law, the question, for me, became: "Does any entity exist that *does* obey Nature's laws, by living in the moment and placing the species' needs above its own?"

In contemplating that question, my civilized mind was introduced to the human spirit, for the first time in my life. It became evident, to me, that the human spirit always lives in the moment, and that it never places its needs above those of our species. In other words, it obeys Nature's laws. How could it not, given that the human spirit is an expression of the forces of Nature that created us?

The spirit's sensibilities are always tied to the moment. We can see it when a couple is madly in love. Those feelings seem eternal, while, unbeknownst to them, they apply only to the moment. Consequently, they provide no clue as to whether the individuals will feel good or bad about each other five weeks, five months, five years, or five decades into the future. The spirit's sensibilities are also visible in the willingness of people to sacrifice even their lives on behalf of others, when the situation calls for it. In such circumstances, we are seeing the spirit placing the species' needs above its own.

Revelations like these had a profound effect on my thinking. My perspective on everything changed when I realized that, while every species changes emotionally and physically, over evolutionary time, no species can survive unless the genetically encoded sensibilities of each given individual remain permanent and unchangeable, from birth. Otherwise, the species' needs would never be served. Indeed, *our* species needs are not presently being served, because of the spiritual repression required to comply with civil law.

That realization led to yet another—that the human spirit needs a spiritual home, a home where we are welcomed as we are, not as a result of pretending we are something we're not. It's a place where life is lived in concert with the forces of Nature that created us, not in defiance of them.

In modern life, since the birth of civilization, spiritual homes have been inaccessible to us, and will remain so, as long as we believe in institutions and their laws. For as long as we stay within this paradigm, we will continue to sacrifice our spiritual lives on the altar of future control.

I've said this, before, but it bears repeating. Though humanity's belief in the law now seems overwhelming, I am convinced the day will come when we will escape our current paradigm. When it comes, I think it will happen swiftly for each individual, like a switch turning on. The Aha! moment will happen when we've reached the point of recognizing that the promise of the law is, in fact, false. Once the spell is broken, we will never again believe in anything the law promises. On that day, there will be only one thing left on this planet, for us to believe in: People! The switch, from believing in the law to believing in people, is the single step we need. A single step will start the transition from legal subjugation to the freedom of a spiritual home.

Something very important will happen, the instant our mind let's go of the illusion that there is any value to our souls in the future promised by wealth and privilege. Our psyches will shed their beliefs, and we will suddenly realize that everything we've spent our lives striving for is meaningless. We'll realize that life's meaning comes through relationships that serve life, not from accomplishing personal goals.

In fact, the worst thing that can happen to anyone who finds meaning in achieving a goal, is to achieve it: After the excitement dies down, the meaning evaporates. In modern life, we are like Sisyphus, perpetually seeking meaning through yet another futile task. Our souls don't care one bit how much wealth we've accumulated, or how many Olympic medals we've won. They care only that we are taking care of life, now, in relationships of mutual dependence. If we are taking care of life, we will experience love and contentment. If we are not, we will remain perennially in search of both.

What does it take for that single first step out of subjugation? What will spark the realization that will detach us from the illusion that we can control our future to a meaningful end? The answer is pain. The unbearable emotional pain of spending our lives trying to fulfill objectives, without receiving the promised rewards, will eventually start the process.

Pain is Nature's carrier of messages and warnings. Through pain, instincts warn all animate beings that they are not serving life. Given natural circumstances, not much pain is required to keep individuals in line. But modern man's existence is not natural. We ignore all sorts of pain, in our effort to control our futures. We suffer the spiritual insult of formal education. We tolerate jobs we don't like. We endure difficult marriage relationships. I mention only a few. To emotionally survive, our minds must numb us to the pain of not taking care of life, by subconsciously accepting, as real, the future promised by our beliefs—religious, ideological, secular, technological, and others. This is how our beliefs trap us: By enabling us to endure the pain of not taking care of life, they facilitate our ability to remain in circumstances in which we are, in fact, not taking care of life. The bottom line for humanity is this: We will remain in this trap until the pain becomes so great that our beliefs can no longer hold it at bay. That is going to take a lot of pain. Meanwhile, as we continue not taking care of life, our circumstances will continue to degrade, until Nature finally delivers enough pain to get us back on track.

This trap was set thousands of years ago, and we did it to ourselves, when men granted themselves the right to own women, through the practice of marriage. It was mankind's first attempt to control the future. That single act destroyed our spiritual homes—our natural "survival units." It destroyed our sisterhoods and brotherhoods—our natural support. Mankind's subsequent plunge into institutional subjugation was swift. No longer able to survive naturally, we immediately became dependent on centralized systems of control—*even to define what a family is*. This led, initially, to the formation of tribal authorities, and—with the advent of the written word—civil ones. But the spiritual homes we lost are the only homes our souls know, and human life on this planet will never feel right—or be safe, again—until we humans go back home.

You see, a spiritual home, is not a place. It is a feeling. When we re-embrace interdependent relationships—relationships of mutual trust—we will *know* we are home, because we will love the people close to us, unconditionally. That is the essence of a spiritual home—not something physical, but something far more significant to our souls.

A spiritual home consists of unbreakable bonds of unconditional love, like the bonds we can only have with our pets, in the present world. Through the contentment we feel, when we finally embrace these bonds, our souls will inform us that we are taking care of life, and that we are again living in concert with our reason for being.

CHAPTER THIRTEEN

Maintaining a Spiritual Home

Nonverbal Communication, the Lifeblood of a Spiritual Home

Spiritual homes occur naturally in a world ruled by the human spirit. But, in our world, ruled by money and law, resurrecting them will not be easy. Many things need to be in place for a spiritual home to exist, things that once fell naturally into place, in the time before centralized systems of authority existed.

To get an idea of how difficult it is to recreate a spiritual home, imagine you are mixing batter for a cake. After the first two or three stirs of the spatula, you decide you don't want to make a cake, after all. You ask yourself: How do I "unstir" the ingredients so I can return them to their original containers? It's not easy. In fact it's virtually impossible. That's precisely what rules, longterm plans, and prescribed commitments do to spiritual homes—they stir the pot. They not only destroy natural social order, but people become dependent on these plans, and these artificially arranged commitments, for their sense of wellbeing. Given the difficulty, we need to recognize that, no matter how much we come to believe we need a spiritual home, it may never happen. If spiritual homes never again form, we'll have to continue depending on the comfort offered by drugs or beliefs, in order to emotionally survive our institutional subjugation.

Though the difficulties are immense, there is reason to believe spiritual homes will someday recur. In my estimation, all 8+ billion of we civilized humans alive, today, need a home where we can be true to ourselves. In the face of that much need, it's hard not to imagine that something will eventually happen, to satisfy it.

But, trying to reconstruct spiritual homes by plan would truly be like trying to unstir the pot. No plan can possibly put all the pieces back in place. What's needed is a reawakening to the needs of our souls. Then, our spirits will lead us back home. So, don't expect to find a set of instructions or plans in this book. This book is about a spiritual reawakening.

Spiritual homes, I caution, are not communes or cults. I believe the motivation of the many people who have taken the radical step of joining communes or cults, over the years, reveals a widespread desire for the intimacy that is so lacking in a world without spiritual homes. Unfortunately, communes and cults have proven they can't provide either stability or intimacy. Of course, they can't! They are as focused as states are on realizing a certain future, through plans and beliefs. They impose the same spiritual dishonesty that states do, thus are just as predisposed to fail—sometimes spectacularly, as in the cases of Jonestown and Waco.

Then, there was the anti-establishment cultural phenomenon of the 60's and 70's that spread throughout the western world. The hippies correctly recognized that the established way of life was founded on a lie, but they did not identify it. The lie on which our modern way of life is based is the belief that the unknowable future can be made knowable by the force of law. Not understanding the essence of the lie, the hippies had no way of life to offer with which to replace the one they were trying to escape. So, they made love life's objective, as if loving by intent could solve our problems. But, to make *anything* an objective, even love, disconnects us from our feelings of the moment, as do the rules and legal commitments they were trying to avoid. Eventually, the flower children found themselves with no choice, other than to again participate in the self-perpetuating lie they had so desired to escape.

Like them, I have no plan to offer, for forming spiritual homes in which people would be free to be true to their feelings of the moment. But I am confident that spiritual homes will begin appearing, organically and spontaneously, once enough people come to recognize that the promise of the law is a lie. When this happens, I am certain that women will be key to forming and maintaining them, because sisterhoods are the core of spiritual homes. Women have a very different kind of emotional intelligence from men. They have a far greater sense that something fundamental about human existence needs to change. What could be more fundamental than to change from family relationships based on legal obligations to families based on spiritual obligations?

> *Unlike masculine power, which is the power to create things that can be controlled, Feminine Power is the power to manifest that which is beyond our control, including those things that our heart most yearns for—intimacy, relatedness, creative expression, authentic community, meaningful contribution, and authentic success.*
>
> —Dr. Jean Houston

Though we can't know, specifically, how spiritual homes will form, I *am* prepared to discuss, in depth, the qualities that sustain a spiritual home. Keep in mind that, though I am quite specific about what's required, I have no experiential evidence for the things I'm about to say. I have never lived in a spiritual home, nor do I know anyone who has. My views are based, not on facts or experience, but on what I have come to believe are the requirements for a spiritually free way of life: Every person's identity and sense of wellbeing must be based on relationships, rather than money, property, plans, or prescribed commitments.

We've been conditioned by our present way of life to believe that, through money, property, and longterm plans, we can realize personal or collective ambitions. But life is a process that is eternally in a state of change. To be spiritually alive, we must participate in the process, not try to use it to our own ends—as occurs universally, under civil rule. Life's process can't be stopped. It goes on with or without us. Personal and collective ambitions separate us from the process, and we immediately get left behind, as will our species, ultimately. In discussing how to maintain spiritual homes, we are addressing nothing less than the crucial question of how we—and eventually our species—can rejoin life's process. It's the only place where our spirits are free to live.

Be forewarned: We are creatures of habit who are steeped in the ways of the institutional paradigm. So, it will be mindblowing to recognize what's required to let go of our designs on the future: It's as shocking as coming home and finding our house burned down. The ways of maintaining a spiritual home are, at first, going to appear totally irrational, irresponsible, silly, impossible, and even ridiculous, from the point of view of the civilized mind. How could they not? The civilized mind believes in institutions, which are founded on the belief that humans are not trustworthy. A spiritual home, on the other hand, is founded on the innate human propensity for spiritual trust—the very antithesis of the modern paradigm.

Institutions do not trust the human spirit. Indeed, their very existence depends on spiritual distrust. Only people have the capacity to trust the human spirit. But, doing so requires action: Sitting on a lounge chair contemplating how trustworthy the human spirit is changes nothing. Crossing the rubicon between our belief-ridden world and the natural human way of life, requires an *act* of trust. It means putting our lives on the line, by contributing everything we now think of as ours—including our paychecks, if we have one—to a viable family, a natural family, a family bonded in spiritual trust. This must be done without any personal accounting, and without promises, legal arrangements, or plans, through which we, or any other members of the family, hope to realize personal or collective designs on the future.

We all know that no individual can survive in the modern world, without a personal store of wealth. It *can* be done, however, by living with others in a spiritual home. In such families, no member's income will go to a personal bank account. It will go to the equivalent of a bowl on the table. That money will be their gift to the family, in return for which they trust that the family will take care of them. They will trust that whoever takes that money will use it to benefit the family and its members. Patterns will form, of course, regarding who typically handles the money, just as they will, regarding how all members choose to serve the family. Limiting access to the money or its management to specific individuals would be an act of spiritual distrust. A spiritual home cannot exist, if its members distrust the human spirit.

With the money accessible to everyone—including those who serve the family in ways other than making money—all members will have to choose between material wealth and spiritual wealth, every day of their lives. But, when living in a state of spiritual wealth, I believe people will choose spiritual wealth over material wealth, every time.

Furthermore, I'm guessing family members will take pleasure in just how much material wealth they can do without, because that will mean there is more there for their sisters and brothers. As social primates, we are born to take care of the people around us, not ourselves. It's simply the way we are. *Taking care of us is the responsibility of those who love us.*

I think what makes Christmas such a special holiday isn't that it's a celebration of Jesus's birth, but that it's a time of giving. As social primates, we evolved to find pleasure in devoting our lives in service to others. During that season of giving, we modern people get a taste of what spiritual freedom feels like. Indeed, because we were born to live lives of mutual dependence, there is no greater spiritual insult that can be visited on human beings than to make each individual personally responsible for their own wellbeing, which is precisely what monetary systems do. A spiritual home relieves us of that spiritual insult, along with countless others, by providing an interdependent way of living.

As for individuals who prove untrustworthy with the money, the human spirit will ferret them out, and the matter will be taken care of, even if it requires shunning. To live in spiritual trust doesn't mean that you trust individuals who have proven untrustworthy.

To maintain spiritual freedom, the family members will avoid organized, formal, or regularly scheduled meetings, and there will be no voting. Both are spiritually repressive relics of hierarchical thinking that have no place in the natural human way of life. Family members will informally gather for meals, celebrations and other events. On occasion, a community, made up of several neighboring families, will join in communal celebration. On more special occasions, possibly annually, the members of several communities might join in festivities.

It's the informality of these gatherings that frees the spirit to communicate the messages that organize the lives of spiritually free people. These messages are conveyed mostly through body language and behavior—virtually none through verbal utterances. Body language is the nonverbal communication that provides a continuous stream of soul-felt information that passes freely between and among family members. All social species—including pre-humans for millions of years, and, more recently, early homo sapiens—have effortlessly formed and maintained family and communal relationships, in this way.

If thirty people are gathered, each individual is aware of the behavior of every other individual who is present. Thus, there are thirty times thirty, or nine hundred nonverbal channels open for communication. This massive amount of communication creates, in effect, a "spiritual gravity field" that unites and organizes the family. Without effort or intent, each individual knows to which family he or she belongs, and *falls* into his or her own soul-felt nitch within it. Through this role, all individuals contribute to the whole, by their own volition.

As a result of this spiritual gravity field, if an individual feels more comfortable with a family other than the current one, then that family will become his or her home. Based on the behavior of other social primates, it's far more likely that males will "gravitate" between families, than females.

The significance of nonverbal communication cannot be overstated, because it is the organizing influence that maintains social order among spiritually free people. Think of it as of equal importance to the flow of blood in a living organism. The spiritual life of a family would instantly die, without its members perceiving the nuances of the ever-shifting feelings being communicated nonverbally, among them.

In modern life, most of us live alone. Even if we don't, we are rarely, if ever, in the presence of thirty or forty people whose lives are of any real significance to our own. Thus, we are largely deprived of meaningful nonverbal communication. As a consequence, we live in a vacuum both spiritual and existential. Like hunting dogs who are never taken on hunts, we languish in a sense of unfulfillment, never knowing how much we are suffering, because, without spiritual homes, we've never had the opportunity to be spiritually alive.

I don't believe people are looking for the meaning of life as much as they are looking for the experience of being alive.

—Joseph Campbell

When we exist without meaningful life experiences, we seek meaning in our imaginations. In fact, our imaginations provide us virtually the only reality we have. Thus, we spend most of our time contemplating the vision of a desired future that resides only in our heads. Our search for meaning and purpose in imagined futures pushes us ever further toward desiring irreconcilable realities. There are people who desire capitalism, a reality in which money owns everything. Others desire communism, a reality in which the state owns everything. There are people who desire a reality in which women have the right to choose, while others desire a reality in which fetuses have the right to live. When such divergences continue to fester, eventually, things reach the point where we desire to kill one another, based on feelings that arise, not from our souls, but from our imaginations. This is how our imaginations, fueled by mankind's unique usage of language inevitably results in revolution, or international conflict. All of this, because, without spiritual homes, reality is what we imagine it to be, rather than what we experience.

What about verbal communication? What role does it play in the life of a spiritual home? In addressing that question, it's important to realize that language, as humans use it, is a very recent development on the evolutionary scale of time. It has existed for only the last two hundred thousand years—.03% of the 600 million years that animate beings have walked upon the surface of this planet.

Speech can be supportive of the life of a spiritual home. But, since it's such a radical and recent phenomenon, it has derailed the normal human evolutionary trajectory, thus has the potential to destroy a spiritual home. Speech can be used in any way you want, as long as it is not used to make rules or longterm plans. Speech supports the home, for instance, when used for sharing soul-felt feelings, or for discussing the location of necessities, like food and water, or agreeing on such things as who will fix breakfast, in the morning.

But, speech enables homo sapiens to do something that non-verbal communication can't—to collectively agree on rules, prescribe commitments, and make longterm plans. These destroy spiritual homes, by separating people from the moment, the only domain in which the human spirit lives. Once a group of people collectively agree on such things as who can have sex with whom, what time the lights go out at night, or who will be responsible for various chores, all members must comply with the prescribed arrangements—or else they are expelled, shamed, or whatever. This forces the members to be spiritually dishonest—to lie about how they feel in the moment, in order to comply with collectively agreed upon arrangements. Unconditional love cannot exist among spiritually dishonest people, even when the dishonesty is imposed by the need to comply with rules. Without love, there is no spiritual home.

How can the family be certain that all the "chores" will be taken care of, without assigning individuals to each task? That's what living in the moment and spiritual trust is about—trusting that when something needs to be taken care of, an individual, or group of individuals, will pitch in and take care of it, of their own volition. There is no such thing as work, in a spiritually free culture. The human spirit sees the effort required to fulfill a need, not as work, but as an opportunity to serve others whom the individual loves.

As civilized people who spend much of our lives doing things we would prefer not to have to do, it might surprise us to realize that people like being occupied. Indeed, having nothing to do is a stressful situation for a human to be in. When we *are* occupied, the question is, are we occupied in obedience to rules and prescribed commitments, in service to our own personal future? Or do we do it of our own volition, in service to people we love? The answer to that question reveals whether or not we're spiritually free.

All rules, longterm plans, and prescribed commitments are based on spiritual distrust. People who do not trust the human spirit have no choice, other than to insist on rules. But, rules impose spiritual dishonesty, thus, lead to spiritual estrangement and eventual disbandment. States, communes, and cults are all rule-based, and this is the reason they eventually disband. States are massive cults which last longer, but only because they are larger—and because it's easier to leave "small cults." When leaving a massive cult, there is nowhere to go, other than to another massive cult.

Nonverbal communication is spiritually honest, because it expresses how we feel in the moment, when we are spiritually free. Anger, in reaction to another's behavior is as natural and essential as love is to the spiritual life of a real home, because both come from the soul. When we tell someone we are angry with them, or love them, we are using speech to express how we feel in the moment—the same thing that body language does. We are being true to ourselves. But, we are not being true to ourselves when we use speech to collectively agree on rules and arrangements. That is something that body language can't do. By dictating the behavior of all who are subject to our prescribed commitments, we are, in effect, playing god. We are introducing the concepts of right or wrong, good and evil. Good people are those who comply with *our* rules and prescriptions, and evil ones are those who don't.

In a spiritual home, voting will be avoided, because, in the act of voting, groups of people are playing God by collectively deciding on what behavior is allowed, that is, what is good or evil. Furthermore, voting inspires scheming and unnatural alliances, which are the seeds of corruption. Even worse, as when our supreme court reaches a five-to-four decision, voting results in the presumption that issues are resolved, when, from the point of view of those who disagree with the decision, things have only been made worse. Allowing unresolved issues to fester will destroy a spiritual home, just as it in-fact destroys nation states.

There are no "shoulds" in a spiritual home—only *what-is,* as revealed by the wisdom of our souls. If someone is angry, they're angry. There is no "they shouldn't be." If a couple is romantically involved, they are romantically involved. There is no "they shouldn't be."

If living in the moment doesn't result in unbreakable bonds, it's a message from our collective souls telling us that the family has become dysfunctional—that it is not serving life. Either there are individuals who don't fit, or the family has become too large. In the first case, the group's collective spirit will identify the ones who don't fit, and the problem will be taken care of. In the second, the family will naturally split, an event that marks the birth of a new family.

The above description depicts how I believe evolutionary wisdom has effortlessly and seamlessly managed social bonding, for millions of years. I caution you again: Don't take it as a set of instructions, or as gospel. *There is no gospel, in Nature, no promised land.* There is only the human spirit, and the moment. The fullness of life is realized in those two dimensions, or it is never realized at all.

My intent, here, is to describe, not prescribe. Don't believe anything I say, because I say it. Believe it only if you understand *why* I say it. These views are not based on facts, but on my belief that if you avoid rules and longterm plans, everything I suggest as essential to sustaining the life of a spiritual home will occur naturally—indeed, unavoidably—without effort or intent. For this, we can thank the human spirit's emotional intelligence.

Of course, skeptics can ask what-if questions ad infinitum, such as, "What if someone absconds with the money?" In that case, the family's reaction would probably be, "Good riddance!"—an expression of relief that the individual is no longer around. With 20 or 30 people contributing, the family would be awash in economic resources, even if most of the contributors worked for minimum wage, thus would be able to weather events of this kind.

All what-if questions about the distant future are invalid, because the future is unknowable. The question to ask isn't what might happen, but: "Do I trust the human spirit?," which is also to ask, "Do I trust the forces of Nature that created us?" The human spirit did not evolve to answer invalid questions. It evolved to subconsciously analyze the complexities of the situation at hand, in far more detail than our conscious minds could ever imagine, and to inspire reactions that serve life.

What-if questions inevitably result in spiritual distrust, because the human spirit has no answers for future uncertainties—nor does any other entity on earth. Any individual who presumes to have such answers is, by definition, illusioned, and is suffering from culturally imposed dementia.

Only spiritual homes can cure culturally imposed dementia, by freeing people to live in the moment. In a spiritual home, we will experience life's real reward, spiritual wealth. I have little doubt that, given the choice between spiritual and material wealth, virtually every human would choose to live in spiritual wealth, even though most people have never experienced it. The presence of spiritual homes in the midst of the modern world, will make it evident, even to present-day humans, that spiritual wealth is available. This could open the floodgates. If that occurs, the circumstances of mankind's existence will transform far more rapidly than we can now imagine.

CHAPTER FOURTEEN

Eternal Life

Beyond our need for the love and contentment of spiritual homes, there are other matters that bear on our need to regain our trust in the human spirit. One is the problem of international conflict. This was brought to my attention recently, when a speaker made the point that we must not allow our passions to get out of hand, as they sometimes do—for example, in late-night bar fights. While the speaker was making that point, a slide appeared on the screen that read, "Don't die over a bad song on the jukebox."

In that moment I was struck by this thought: Could that be what all our ideologies are, these high-minded religiously held dogmas that we moderns allow to rule our lives, and which we so passionately kill and die for? Are they merely "bad songs on a jukebox?" If so, then this worldwide struggle for ideological supremacy that all humans alive today have inherited, is nothing more than a massive late-night bar fight. How can we return to our senses, so we can stop the fight?

I wish the psychiatrists and social scientists were further along in their fields than they seem to be. We need, in a hurry, some professionals who can tell us what has gone wrong in the minds of the statesmen in this generation.

How is it possible for so many people with the outward appearance of steadiness and authority, intelligent and convincing enough to have reached the highest positions in the governments of the world, to have lost so completely their sense of responsibility for the human beings to whom they are accountable? Their obsession with stockpiling nuclear armaments and their urgency in laying out detailed plans for using them have, at the core, aspects of what we would be calling craziness in other people, under other circumstances. Just before they let fly everything at their disposal, and this uniquely intelligent species begins to go down, it would be a small comfort to understand how it happened to happen. Our descendants, if there are any, will surely want to know.

—Lewis Thomas: "Craziness" from the book: *Late Night Thoughts on Listening to Mahler's Ninth Symphony*

Spiritually free people will engage in armed conflict over territorial disputes, from time to time, or they may do it for no other reason than the sport of it—i.e., for practice. That's natural. But spiritually free people will not engage in armed conflict over ideological supremacy, nor will their conflicts threaten life on earth, which would be craziness. To cure this collective madness requires spiritual trust, something that no government can offer, or encourage. Indeed, governments preach spiritual *distrust,* because their very existence depends on their subjects distrusting the human spirit.

It's one way or the other: We make this transition to trusting the human spirit, or we remain forever frozen in the madness of spiritual isolation, a madness that is reflected, not only in international conflicts, but worldwide habitat destruction. We've lived in a state of madness since humans first began entertaining "what-if" questions about the future, thousands of years ago.

Convinced that we have rational answers to all what-if questions, modern humans presume to be in control of life. Therefore, we believe we have the power to make the world a better place. But, from our spirit's point of view, the world doesn't need to be made better. So, you can't realize life's meaning by trying to do that. Life's meaning can only be felt and understood by being who we are and reacting to how things are:

> *How many of you want more love, intimacy, joy? True belonging doesn't require you to change who you are. It requires you to be who you are. You don't measure vulnerability by the amount of disclosure. Like tweeting your bikini wax: not vulnerability. I'm not going to bullshit you. Vulnerability is hard, and it's scary, and it feels dangerous. But it's not as hard or scary or dangerous as getting to the end of our lives and having to ask ourselves, "What if I had shown up?"*
>
> —Brené Brown: "The Call to Courage"

I would love to tell you that we can be vulnerable, and therefore experience sisterhood and brotherhood, while maintaining a personal store of wealth. It would make my arguments on behalf of spiritual freedom far more palatable. If I could tell you that, and then invent a rationale to "prove" it, I might have a best seller on my hands. After all, who doesn't want to have their cake and eat it too?

But I'm not going to bullshit you, either. What is the hardest, scariest, most dangerous thing we can imagine doing in a culture where access to everything we need for survival has a price on it? It would be to surrender our personal wealth. Indeed, given our present circumstances, we would be fools to do so. So, we must take care not to blame ourselves, or anyone else, if nobody ever does it.

But, surrendering our personal wealth is precisely what must occur, if we are ever to "be who we are." As long as we depend on personal stores of wealth to survive, we will remain agents of the state. We'll live out our entire lives never knowing the answer to the question, "What if I had shown up?" By placing our trust in our sisters and brothers, on the other hand, we can break our dependence on personal wealth, thus gain the freedom to become agents of life by fulfilling our spiritual obligations to each other.

In the world where everyone must depend on personal wealth to survive, no one can ever know sisterly and brotherly love, because spiritual obligations and the interdependent relationships that go with them make no sense in a world where success is defined by wealth and privilege. That is the crux of the intimacy issue for civilized man: Only by fulfilling our spiritual obligations do we reveal our inborn need for one another, thus also our love for one another.

Love is not a matter of choice. It happens in circumstances of mutual dependence. You can't love others, if you don't need them. To love others, absent need, is to pretend love. Indeed, the intensity of our love for others is directly proportional to the intensity of our need for them. If you are dependent on others to *survive*, then your love for them is unconditional.

We don't love people because they need us. We love them because *we need them*. Love is not something we do. It's something we need.

The documentary, "Restrepo," reveals the relationship between interdependence and unconditional love, through the eyes of battlefield soldiers in Afghanistan. In a scene from an interview taken at Restrepo, the remote military outpost where they were serving, a soldier described how the members of his platoon felt about one another.

"They're the best guys that you could ever be with. Even the guys you don't like, you love them, you know. Even the guys you fight with, you argue with, you'll die for. So how much can you hate them. Talk about dudes that, you know, work together and you'd think after 13 months you'd start to fall apart. But the truth is, it's only brought us closer."

—Brendan O'Byrne

Our modern desire for personal wealth results from our unnatural concern about the future, which is a consequence of existing without the love inherent to spiritual homes. The future is unknowable. It's pointless for any living being to worry about it. That's why it was inevitable that animate beings would evolve to live in the moment, and why the soldiers in Restrepo experienced unconditional love. Their utter dependence on one another for survival placed them in the moment.

Only a few aspects of the future need concern any animate being—the recurring ones, like the coming of darkness, or the changing of the seasons.

When Jesus implored us to take care of one another, in the now, and let the future take care of itself, he was telling us something that our human spirits have always known. But the way of life created by our indoctrinated selves has rendered us so dissociated from our innate wisdom that we have scant access to what we really know.

Sensing that what Jesus said was profound, we worshipped him as God—the creator of the universe, manifest. But our indoctrinated selves did not realize why his words were profound. We didn't understand that he was revealing to us the wisdom of our own souls. So, humanity went right on trusting our futures to personal stores of wealth, rules, and plans, as if he had never existed. Never, since then, have we embraced the idea of being true to our souls, as he implored us to do.

Though Jesus was right, the fact that the future will take care of itself doesn't mean that living in the moment would enable people to survive anything the future might throw at them. It means that people living in a spiritual home *feel confident* that they can manage all future uncertainties, because their sisters and brothers are by their side. That is key. How we feel is the only thing that matters from our real self's point of view. Even death has no sting for an individual who places his or her life on the line, on behalf of others. Soldiers throw themselves on live grenades to save their buddies. Mothers risk drowning or fire to save their children. In these ultimate expressions of unconditional love, the "real self" experiences sacrifice as the ultimate emotional high.

You see, life *is* a risk, and our real selves evolved to celebrate it. Without risk, we would have no need for one another, no need for intimacy, no need for a spiritual home.

Interdependent relationships are significant because, through the pleasure we experience when serving one another, we are relieved of anxiety. When attending to needs that transcend our own existence, our lives become transcendent, because we are serving a purpose that exists beyond us. In essence, our lives become eternal, because they are invested in the wellbeing of life, not in the wellbeing of self. This results in lives that are free of the fear of failure, or of death.

Contrast that with an independent way of life—the measure of success in a world without spiritual homes. We may achieve the wealth required to bathe ourselves in luxuries, but whatever pleasure we experience is in service to self. A life that is not serving needs that transcend its own existence is meaningless to our spirits. If our real selves find no meaning in our existence, then our indoctrinated selves will be hard pressed to find meaning in it, other than through devotion to beliefs and other illusions about how the world or the hereafter are supposed to be.

Without the mutual support of a spiritual home, you see, fear is our default emotion—fear of failure, fear of the future, fear of death. Fear defines us, which enables ideologies, institutions, religions, and other illusions of security to have their way with us.

What it all boils down to is this question: Do we want to spend our lives accumulating material wealth in service to an indoctrinated self, whose sensibilities are grounded in fear? Or do we want to place our trust in the human spirit, and live in a state of spiritual wealth?

Our current paradigm gives us no choice but to pursue material wealth. If the paradigm ever changes, it will happen when people begin to understand how the current untenable paradigm came to be. That understanding will release our spirits to guide us back to spiritual homes and the spiritual wealth of the natural human way of life.

The good news is that, even a small group of people can make the transformation. To know sisterhood and brotherhood, we don't have to wait for everyone on earth to see through the illusion of future control that currently obliterates normal human relationships. Twenty or thirty people who believe in the human spirit can make the transformation to a spiritual home, by joining in a sisterhood and brotherhood of mutual trust. Though humankind is presently lost in the illusion of future control, that doesn't mean that we, as a body of people living in spiritual trust, must remain lost.

CHAPTER FIFTEEN

Life is Not Being Taken Care Of

A Message from Nature, Delivered by the Female Soul

The core of a spiritual home is a sisterhood. By that I mean that the family's existence is dependent upon the existence of the sisterhood, and the collective sensibilities of the sisterhood have absolute authority within the family. Sex plays no role in family bonding. Sex is for procreation inspired by feelings of romance, which might even occur between individuals from different families. Within naturally bonded human families, paternity is unknown.

Charlize Theron—an acclaimed actress and one of Glamor Magazine's 2019 women of the year, was interviewed by the Me-To movement about female empowerment. When asked if she had ever had a "me-to" experience, Theron made what was, for me, a profound statement about the circumstances of women in modern life: "Yes, I think it's important for us to talk about the wide spectrum of that. It's when you sit in a room and feel like you have to placate somebody of the opposite sex, or to make them feel better or to laugh at their jokes or to make yourself a little smaller in order for everything to just be smooth. I think those are things that every woman can relate to."

The empowerment of women is the most important advancement towards spiritual freedom taking place in the world, today. The most devastating thing that can happen to any social species is for the females to have to play second fiddle to the males. That is what has been happening to our species since the introduction of marriage allowed men to own women, thousands of years ago. Not only have women knowingly shrunk themselves in the presence of men, so that we men could enjoy whatever privileges of ownership we think are due us, but women have had to depend on the state to protect them and their children from men—a responsibility no state can fulfill.

In the most advanced nations on earth, there is widespread child trafficking, sexual abuse of children by family members, physical and emotional abuse of children by their fathers, and physical abuse of women by their spouses. This is to say nothing of what is probably the most insidious and prevalent spiritual offense of all: *Women must hide their real feelings, to sustain the appearance of order.* This comment was inspired by Theron's remarks, but inspired even more by the life of my dear mother. During the prime years of her life, she hid almost every real feeling she had, in order to manage a married situation which, from all outward appearances, was quite normal. But she suffered, a suffering that no one else even realized was going on, until years later, when she shared her real feelings with my then wife, Joyce, during family visits. I do not disparage my father, or any of the family members involved, for what my mother endured. On behalf of my father, I want to make it clear that he was an exemplary man, deeply respected my mother, and never physically or emotionally abused her. She suffered for the same reason women across the face of this planet have been suffering for thousands of years. They have had to subjugate themselves to the contract of marriage, in order to have a family and children—and, largely, must do so, even today.

When will the suffering stop? It will stop when women quit believing in the promises of men: *If you just keep your faith in our institutions, laws, and legal arrangements, everything will work out fine.*

It was not always this way. Before civilization was invented, each sex played their natural role in serving life. Evolution commissioned women to be life's caretakers, and men to be its protectors. Far more emotional intelligence is required to take care of life, than to protect it, which is why women must make themselves "a little smaller in order for everything to just be smooth," particularly in a male dominated culture. Little wonder that my mother, and billions of others, have felt compelled to hide their real feelings in a world in which taking care of legal imperatives is infinitely more important than taking care of life.

As the modern world faces crisis after crisis, for which there are no proven answers, there is ever greater reason for women to cease believing in the promises of men. Freed of men's promises, women will naturally gravitate together, as sisterhoods. When functioning as sisterhoods, they will regain their long-lost spiritual authority to cele-brate life the way social primate females have always celebrated life—*by taking care of it.* This must occur before humanity is overwhelmed by the mountain of problems that face us, and for which we men can only offer imagined solutions.

Having regained their natural role, women will never again feel the need to spiritually shrink before anyone, and they and their chil-dren will be safe from men. Men will still play an important role in their lives, as their lovers, supporters, and protectors. But men will no longer abuse anyone. Imagine what would happen if a man sexually or physically abused one of the sisters or her child. He would be lucky to escape alive, and it's the brothers, themselves, who would take care of the matter.

No social species can long endure, without viable families, in which the members serve life through their service to one another. The human species is no exception.

The idea that women should look to one another to form the core of a spiritual home strikes many as so odd that they wonder why I would suggest such a thing. I say it because the practice of men owning women isn't viable, and the fact that men have been doing it for thousands of years, doesn't make it so.

By comparison, it's been only about one hundred fifty years since women began to gain civil rights—and with those rights, the freedom to function independently of men. It is most interesting and instructive to note that the principal argument men used against women being given civil rights was that women are "emotional creatures" incapable of making rational choices. The fear was that, if women were allowed to function independently of men, it would destroy the family structure on which the very idea of civilization stands.

That fear is being realized. During the short time that women have had civil rights, the institutionalized order on which humans have based family relationships for thousands of years has essentially broken down. We see the effects of this breakdown in the form of overcrowded abuse shelters, high divorce rates, and the fact that over half of American adults now live alone.

What men overlooked, when they decided to own women—at the peril of mankind—is that life has the greater say. Mankind's natural way of life and the family relationships in which it is grounded, cannot be held at bay, forever—certainly not by the flawed human belief in "rational" moral laws that ushered in modern cultures. The idea that humanity can survive indefinitely by complying with manmade laws predisposes all modern cultures to failure.

Civilizations fail, because *life is not the rational process* governments presume it to be. How can it be rational? There is no *reason* that renders it axiomatic that life should exist. Throughout the history of civilization, people have tried, and failed, to find that reason. We don't know why the universe exists, or what sparked the appearance of life on earth. These things are not for us to know—nor does it matter. All our attempts to explain them rationally are nothing more than speculations, wishes, and beliefs—parts and pieces of the massive skein of illusions that blankets our lives, and which we have little choice other than to embrace.

Though we don't know why life exists, it seems fairly clear why beliefs exist: The promises of beliefs make it possible for us to tolerate the spiritual repression imposed on us by the institutions that rule our lives.

When I was a teenager, I could not grasp why my mother believed that the moon produced its own light, as the bible says, instead of what's obvious to the naked eye—that it is illuminated by the sun. Now I understand. Without the afterlife promised by her religion, my mother could never have emotionally survived the spiritual abuse imposed on her by the institution of marriage.

What wasn't obvious to me, then, is that her blindness to the fact that the moon is illuminated by the sun was directly related to the belief in the afterlife, upon which her emotional health depended.

My mother's blindness to evidence that would refute her belief in a better tomorrow, in her case, an afterlife, is not characteristic of normal—spiritually free—human behavior. Spiritually free people live in the moment. They have no beliefs. The only things they perceive as real are the things they have learned from experience. My mother suffered the same blindness as do all civilized people, because it is imposed by institutional subjugation.

Whenever people must deny their feelings of the moment, in order to physically and materially survive the demands placed on us by civil rule, they suffer. To find relief from that suffering, the subconscious mind takes what comfort it can from belief in a better tomorrow. Consequently, the subconscious mind has no choice, other than to blind the conscious mind to any and all evidence that the "better future" promised by our beliefs in money, law, institutions, ideologies, and religion, are not true.

Any way of life justified by rational arguments is doomed to fail, because it stands in contradiction to the forces of life. Those forces are fueled by the instinctive emotional imperatives required for life to go on. Of the freedoms gained by women in the last 150 years, the most significant is their freedom to function independently of men, because it is hastening the demise of our rationally based way of life.

To grasp the significance of women in the overall scheme of things, let us again focus, for a bit, on the significance of emotions. From the beginning of our evolutionary history, emotions have been central to human existence, just as they are central to the existence of any species. Without emotions, there would be nothing to animate us. Every bit as much as our arms and legs, feelings are the artifacts, the evidence, the very expressions of evolution.

Emotion, not reason, is the foundation on which animate life stands. There is nothing rational about love, anger, empathy, romance, beauty, or even hunger—all of which are feelings. And, these feelings, as every human "knows," are the very stuff of consciousness. In fact, without feelings to infuse the objective world with values, there would be nothing to think about. In other words, it's really "I *feel*, therefore

I am," not "I think, therefore I am. A robot can think. But, without feelings to assign values, a robot isn't conscious. It has no clue that it exists, even if programmed to appear that it knows.

Returning to our discussion about the significance of women, when society diminishes women, as emotional creatures, what is really being said is that women are far more likely than men to be true to their feelings of the moment, than to be "reasonable." But, given that feelings are the foundation on which life stands, the fact that women tend to value feelings more than "what's expected," *is their strength*, not their weakness.

Modern human life contradicts mankind's natural way of life—in which women are life's caretakers, men its protectors—in a way that is particularly offensive to the female spirit. Modern women are not free to help each other take care of life, according to the sensibilities of their souls. They must comply with institutional society—a male-ordained way of life based on reason.

Intellectually, *no one knows what's wrong*. But, the female *soul* knows something is *terribly* wrong. As evolution's caretaker of life, the female soul knows that the social order required to sustain human life does not exist—not here, not now. As subjects of moral edicts, women have no choice other than to pretend all is well, even though their souls know it isn't. But, at intervals, their souls simply go ballistic—the organism's only means of restoring emotional equilibrium, and the reason men see women as hysterical creatures whose emotions cannot be trusted.

In this world ruled by rational laws, is it any wonder there is a history of women being accused of irrationality—even burnt at the stake, for madness? Instead of shaming women, we need to celebrate the fact that, on occasion, a female's spirit breaks through the powerful inhibitions of modern life to express the elemental wisdom of her soul. Mankind needs to appreciate the significance of the sometimes-incomprehensible behavior of women, because it carries a profound message straight from Nature. The message is plain and simple: *Life is not being taken care of!*

When belief in institutionalized family relationships finally collapses—as it must, if human life is to go on—women will respond by forming the natural sisterly bonds that result in viable homes for bearing and raising their children. That seachange in family relationships will allow them, and the men who join them, to again function as the social primates that humans are.

In the act of regaining their spiritual authority, sisterhoods will form the core of homes in which men, too, will regain *their* spiritual authority. Through the brotherhoods that will instinctively form, men will reclaim their long-lost natural purpose—to support the sisterhoods. They will end the practice of creating and operating institutions, based on the presumption that men hold dominion over all life on earth—including, until recently, women. Men will once-again have something *real* to die for—the sisterhoods and their children—and nevermore the beliefs and ideologies through which we now justify the existence of legal and monetary systems.

But, the most important change that will result from women regaining their spiritual authority is that they will no longer be subservient to men. In our rediscovered spiritual homes, life will again be taken care of, after thousands of years of abject neglect.

CHAPTER SIXTEEN

Sisterhood, the Hope for Mankind

When I was studying the lions in Africa, I would watch a pride of females who had known each other their entire lives, playing and tumbling with each other's cubs in the late afternoon. And it made me think about my girlfriends back home, and how much I missed them. As primate human females, we have a strong genetic propensity to live in a group. We came from the wild. If we study the wilderness and learn about Nature, we can learn a lot about ourselves.

—Delia Owens, speaking about her bestselling book,
Where the Crawdads Sing.

Relationships have become problematic in the modern world, and I believe Owens's quote points us in the direction of the answer. It's my view that the lions Owens enjoyed watching were experiencing as much contentment as is possible for any living being. I think Owens is right: If we study Nature, we can learn a lot about ourselves. We would learn that "primate females have a strong genetic propensity to live in a group," and that, humans, as social primates, naturally live in extended families. Physical evidence for this is provided by Stanford

University Professor Robert Sapolsky in his "Great Courses" course, "Biology and Human Behavior:" (I Paraphrase)

There are more than 150 species of primates. In each one, the size of the cortex [the part of the brain in which the highest levels of mental functioning occur] correlates with the number of individuals that make up the typical social group for that species. The larger the social group, the larger the cortex. What is the cortex all about, in primates? *It's about social intelligence.*

There is a clear implication to this quote. We humans have the largest brains among all the primates, thus, early on—when we were living in our natural state—we not only bonded in social groups, but our groups were larger than those of any other social primate.

So, here we are, possessed with an emotional intelligence that evolved to manage intimate relationships with as many as 50 to 60 individuals. Yet, for the thousands of years since humans invented civilization, we have been living alone or in pairs. Can you imagine the spiritual insult of it all? I think this insult has a lot to do with how much Owens missed her girlfriends, as well as with the problems civilized people have with relationships, in general.

Relationships have become so problematic in the modern world, that if you are an adult American, you are more likely than not living alone. Our family relationships are so difficult that it is generally accepted that even "successful" ones must be "worked at." This is revealed every time a female public figure is congratulated for the success of her marriage, and replies, "Thanks, but it's not easy. We had to work at it."

So difficult are our present-day relationships that an interstellar visitor might easily conclude that relationships are not part of the human repertoire. This is not anyone's fault. The problem is that sisterhoods are not acceptable in modern cultures, thus we must make do, without them. That is why contentment in relationships is so rare for present-day humans. We lack the sisterhoods that once formed the core, the glue that joined a natural human family into an organic whole. Our innate "social intelligence" recognizes that legally imposed relationships are not natural. Consequently, our spirits are unable to find lasting contentment in them—or, worse, they revolt through divorce or violence.

It is a universal law of Nature that all animate beings—including humans—experience the contentment of unconditional love in the relationships through which they serve life. Humans living in the natural world experience all three forms of unconditional love. Motherly love rewards women for nurturing their young. Romantic love, rewards couples for procreating. And sisterly-brotherly love rewards both men and women for participating in the life of a natural family. Through sisterhood and brotherhood, humans naturally fulfill their spiritual obligation to take care of life, by serving one another.

Sisterly-brotherly love does not exist in the modern world. Nature is out of the picture. Modern humans are bereft of the natural spiritual obligations, without which our lives are meaningless. In the modern family, we answer exclusively to legal obligations that exist to serve the state. Thus, we live our entire lives without ever experiencing what our spirits most crave—the contentment of sisterhood and brotherhood.

This is not a situation that can be rectified swiftly, but I predict that mankind will be liberated from our present situation, eventually. Indeed, the liberation is already in progress. It began in 1839, when Mississippi became the first state in the union to allow women to own property in their own names. Though no one recognized it, this act lifted women from the legal status of slaves, giving them the freedom to function independently of men for the first time since men had invented marriage, thousands of years ago. Throughout history, to be a slave has been to be denied the right to own property. Denial of the right to own property is the circumstance common to all slaves, regardless of race, creed, color, or sex. All women were denied that right, until that Mississippi law was passed. Yet, to this day, no one has recognized how significant it was. It was the first law that lifted women from abject slavery, by giving them the right to own property. If the import of that act is ever recognized, the date of its enactment may go down as the most important one in history.

We are touching on a history of unintended human trials and tribulations that is very long. Even in pre-civilized cultures, it was the repression of female sensibilities, through marriage, that destroyed sisterhoods and brotherhoods, in the first place.

Why would men want to own women, through marriage, if it destroys sisterhood and brotherhood? There was nothing to stop them because they, and the women they were claiming as property, were oblivious to the consequences of men granting themselves the right to own women. Before anyone owned anyone, living as sisterhoods and brotherhoods was a given. It was as natural as breathing. No one imagined that our natural way of life could be destroyed.

We can't know why men decided they wanted to own women, but there are a number of reasons the practice could have begun. Most likely, marriage came into being when humans recognized the connection between sex and childbirth. Men wanted to own their progeny, which required that they own the mother. Or it may have been men's attempt to perpetuate the experience of romance, for life. Or, perhaps men sought social status by owning women.

Whatever the reason men decided they wanted to own women, our human instincts provide no sensibilities that justify the practice. So, to establish that "right," groups of men had to agree that something gave them that right—whether it be God, the powers that be, or something else. To exercise their newly found "God-given" right to own women, they agreed upon a system of rules, and punishments to enforce them. That was the prototype for the first tribal authorities and, eventually—with the advent of the written word—the modern state.

There came a time, after men had established they had the right to own women, that they decided they also had the right to own land, animals, and slaves. That's when humans began building temples to glorify kings, gods, or whatever they believed had given them rights of ownership. The construction of the earliest temples, which occurred around 8 to 10 thousand years ago, marks the institutionalization of men's right to claim land, animals and people, as property. It also coincides with the beginning of civil rule. All systems of social order—including the modern human family—have since been founded on rights of ownership, whether state or private.

In the natural world that existed before men claimed the right to own women, our lives were ruled by the human spirit. There were no human rights—no right to own things, not even the right to live on earth. Our *ability* to live on earth depended on being socially accepted by the members of a natural family. But that all changed, with the advent of civil rule. Since then, our social acceptability has had little to do with our sense of wellbeing. Instead of social values being the key to survival, the state now grants us citizenship at the moment of birth. Through citizenship, we gain the "right" to live on earth. To maintain our "human rights," we are each rendered personally accountable to the dictates of the ideologies or religions upon which the state is founded. This is the price we pay for having lost our sisterhoods. It is one hell of a price!

How long, in evolutionary time, have we been paying this price? If we were to visualize the 600 million years living beings have walked upon the earth as the length of one football field, then, homo sapiens would be seen to have appeared a mere 1.2 inches ago, and the earliest temples fifty-four one-thousandths of an inch ago. Thus, in evolutionary time, the phenomenon of ownership is of no significance, just a flash in the pan. Yet, it destroyed sisterhoods and brotherhoods from the very beginning, and is now threatening to destroy the life of the human species.

But things are changing. In the 180 years—one-thousandth of an inch on our football field—since the moment that women began acquiring the ability to function independently of men, it has become increasingly clear that the institutionalized family does not satisfy the human need for relationships. Unfortunately, this failure remains generally unrecognized. But that won't last long, because the most elemental need of any species is to support its members when they are most vulnerable—when they are young. Social primates evolved to do that by functioning as extended families, of which women form the core.

As a result of the institutionalized family's ongoing failure to satisfy basic human needs—particularly our children's—modern women will soon find themselves forming sisterhoods, again, and for the same reason women evolved to do so—to create safe and secure homes in which to bear and raise their children. The return of sisterhoods will restore female spiritual authority, the foundation for order in natural human families. In doing this, they will literally re-set human life for the people involved, saving them all—men, women, and children, alike—from the emotional nightmare mankind has endured, since we institutionalized human relationships, thousands of years ago.

But, the formation of sisterhoods will result in a conflict with the state, regarding the issue of sovereignty. The sovereignty of a state requires that its authority over each individual be absolute. Once sisterhoods begin forming, conflict with the government will be inevitable, because two sovereigns cannot simultaneously exist. Until the population generally recognizes the spiritual authority of sisterhoods, as sovereign, sisterhoods and their supporting brotherhoods must expect interference from the state.

Clearly, the physical power of a sisterhood is miniscule, compared to the might of a state. This would seem to preclude the possibility that sisterhoods could prevail. Indeed, when I think of a sisterhood standing up against the state, I am reminded of the Tiananmen Square incident, in which a man in China stood up against a column of battle tanks.

In its struggle with sisterhoods, however, the state will face a phenomenon that no state has ever encountered, before—*the spiritual authority of sisterhoods,* which is both elemental and immense. Immense, because sisterhoods are the sole maintainers of order among spiritually free humans. By contrast, no individual, man or woman, is capable of serving the species when functioning alone. Consequently, individuals have very little spiritual authority, making them easy for states to ignore. Indeed, it's because it's so easy for states to ignore the spiritual authority of individuals that states exist.

But a sisterhood is an entirely different thing. Its authority is not derived from weapons that kill and destroy. It comes from the depths of power that reside in the human soul. In our present state of spiritual repression, we don't realize it, but our souls know that, absent sisterhoods, human existence is without meaning, purpose, form, or direction. Furthermore, when dealing with a sisterhood, the state is not dealing with just one individual. It is dealing with a group of women tightly bonded by the natural female propensity to share feelings—a propensity that is trivialized in modern culture. Through such sharing, each of the women knows precisely how the others feel, so, when one of them speaks, she speaks for them all.

Here is a scenario to help visualize how the struggle between a sisterhood and a state might unfold: Imagine that a member of a family feels unfairly treated by the family, and seeks redress through the powers of the state. When confronted by the state, one of the sisters will inform its agent: "You have no business here. If you insist that you do, then imprison us all and institutionalize our children. Otherwise, leave us alone."

With that message, for the first time in history, a state will be faced with the spiritual power of a sisterhood. Though there may be some sacrifices along the way, I am counting on sisterhoods to eventually win that struggle. Any state that tries to solve a problem, social or otherwise, by separating mothers from their children does not recognize how things *are*. If a state did do this, the act would offend the emotional intelligence of every man and woman alive. Sisterhoods, alone, possess the power to confront a state with reality. For this reason, I predict that, when sisterhoods begin forming, their spiritual authority will eventually prove fatal to states. This prediction is the embodiment of my hope for the future of mankind.

Question: Once sisterhoods are recognized as sovereign, what would prevent them from behaving like states, which engage in endless struggles for ideological and territorial supremacy? Answer: Spiritually free people live in the moment—there are no ideologies. Just as importantly, females are not driven to power or self-aggrandizement, through conquest. To differentiate between women and men, regarding the matter of conflict, let's begin by considering the following remarks by Admiral William H McRaven in his book, *Sea Stories*.

As terrible as it sounds, every SEAL longs for a worthy fight, a battle of convictions, and an honorable war. War challenges your manhood. It reaffirms your courage. It sets you apart from the timid souls and the bench sitters. It builds unbreakable bonds among your fellow warriors. It gives your life meaning. Over time, I would get more than my fair share of war. Men would be lost. Innocents would be killed. Families would be forever changed. But somehow, inexplicably, war would never lose its allure. To the warrior, peace has no memories, no milestones, no adventures, no heroic deaths, no gut-wrenching sorrow, no jubilation, no remorse, no repentance, and no salvation. Peace was meant for some people, but probably not for me.

My inclusion of these words is not intended to disparage a truly honorable man. Nor is it intended to disparage men, in general. I use Admiral McRaven's words to remind us that most men are born warriors, though most modern men don't realize it. In truth, men's identity for the last six thousand years has rested largely in their desire to conquer and reorganize life.

Whether we realize it or not, most men find immense satisfaction in conflict. Given the destructive power of modern weapons, mankind now faces the existential threat of self-extinction, as a result of men's love of war. Only sisterhoods have the power to save humanity from this male predisposition to fight. They will do it when they reclaim their natural authority over how and when men perform their natural role as warriors.

In contrast, women are territorial beings—territorial in the way lion prides are. As territorial beings, they will never claim more territory than they need to sustain their families—or community of families. Just as importantly, territorial beings are genetically predisposed to respect the territory of others. What would a sisterhood do with more territory than it needs? Not only would the excess resources be useless to it, but, for that very reason, the claim would not be respected by neighboring communities, making it costly to defend, in terms of effort and lives lost.

As for the brotherhoods, they exist to serve the sisterhoods. Men are the warriors. But should a brotherhood take too much pleasure in armed conflict, as many men now do, in service to failed governments around the world—and, most importantly, should they engage in it without the sisterhoods' blessing—they would find themselves in more trouble at home than they could get into on the battlefield. Death is the worst thing that can happen to a man on the field of battle. But the sisters have the spiritual authority to make the men *wish* they were dead. Their concern would be that the men have gone and stirred up needless trouble that may well come back to haunt the family.

You see, states can exercise control, but only on behalf of idealized futures. Women are born to exercise control on behalf of life. This is the reason I see sisterhoods as the hope for mankind.

CHAPTER SEVENTEEN

Selflessness

When we all live a self-centered existence then what that means is that I am the center of the universe, you're the peripheral, and you're expendable. And if we all live that way, we don't even have a society. Human community, human survival, human life on this planet depends on our capacity to be unselfish, to be selfless and giving. And the miracle is that when we do that, we actually get blessed, ourselves.

—Bishop Michael Curry on *"The Power of Love"*

Bishop Curry is not the only religious leader who has expressed ideas on selflessness that summarize the views contained in this book. Rev. Andy Stanly notes that researchers all over the world are finding a connection between selflessness and happiness. Stanly said, "According to this research, as long as your life is all about *you*, you can't be happy. You could have everything you can imagine you would ever want—this person's looks, that person's intelligence, another person's car, home, wealth, talent, etc. Even with all that," he said, "you still wouldn't be happy. To be happy, the research concludes, you must give your life away in service to others. You must embrace all the New Testament values that we naturally resist—love one another, care for one another, serve one another, forgive one another, carry one another's burdens. Giving our life in service to others is our *only* path to happiness."

This is true, he says, because of "Grand Design"—because of how God made us. With all due respect, on this point I disagree with Stanly. As I see it, the forces of Nature created us. In my view, God and Nature are one and the same. Thus, I would prefer to say that, to be happy, we need to serve others, because of how Nature made us.

I also disagree with Stanly's view that people are naturally resistant to the things Jesus told us to do. Quite the opposite. When people face natural disasters or armed conflict together, they readily give their all on behalf of those around them. In doing so, they are amply rewarded, by Nature/God, with love for one another. Consider these testimonies of people who have been at war:

> *"I've never felt that close to anyone, I mean not even that close to my wife, compared to the love I had for my brothers."*
>
> – Ron Dorsey

> *"I loved those people as though we were birthed from the same parents. We've seen and done and been through a lot of stuff together, that not even my biological family could understand."*
>
> – Lisa Crutch

> *"That's a fate worse than death, to get into combat and let down the guys who trust you, your buddies. To let them down is worse than any death I can imagine."*
>
> – Dennis Mosly

The connection between interdependence and love was also revealed by Quarterback Kurt Warner, in his remarks when retiring from the National Football League:

"One thing you know is that you are always going to miss Sunday afternoons for a few hours but—my wife and I have talked about it— the thing you are probably going to miss more than anything is the five or six hours a day that you spend in that locker room with those guys. They become your extended family."

We often hear sentiments like Warner's expressed, for example, by cast members of TV shows, years after a series has been discontinued. It isn't the money, the notoriety, or the glory they miss, but the group of people with whom they shared intimacy.

Intimacy is love. But, not all love is unconditional. Any time people have joined together to accomplish something they can't do alone, they will experience love, but of a different level. We see this kind of love in groups like Bridge players, television cast members, and members of football teams. When it's their need to *survive* that has brought people together, however, the intimacy they experience rises to the level of *unconditional love*. This is the state of sisterly and brotherly love that pre-humans, then primitive humans, experienced every day of their lives, in the natural world. Modern humans experience the unconditional love of brotherhood, as soldiers in combat, though it is not war, itself, but the interdependence of surviving war together, which is key to experiencing unconditional love, in that context.

In modern life, precious little unconditional love is ever experienced. So little, in fact, that there are many who argue it doesn't exist. But, it was the key element of human joy, satisfaction and contentment among pre- and primitive humans, who—unlike us—lived the natural human way of life. As social primates, it is our nature to live in sisterhood and brotherhood. In fact, no individual human, or any other social primate, can survive the natural world, alone. The unconditional love that is intrinsic to sisterhoods and brotherhoods in the natural human way of life is the essential ingredient to the survival of any member of a social species.

Stanly asserts that we humans naturally resist the values Jesus talked about. It certainly seems that way. But, I think our resistance has everything to do with our circumstances, and nothing to do with how Nature made us. Nature created us to live in a world ruled by the human spirit. But money rules *our* world. A monetary system renders us each exclusively responsible for our own wellbeing. In *our* world, "success" is independence, not interdependence. To succeed is to prove that we are *not dependent* on others for survival. *How much further could we possibly have strayed from our natural way of being?*

Keep in mind, love is circumstantial. We don't love others because they need us. We love them because we need them. Everyone loves everyone unconditionally, in relationships of mutual dependence, because they need each other, to survive. Given these "circumstances of unconditional love," as I have just defined them, it's clear to see that life is about the wellbeing of our sisters and brothers, never about self. In taking care of us, our sisters and brothers embrace the same spiritual obligation we do.

On the other hand, when we depend on money and property to survive, we don't need anyone, and no one needs us. Consequently, we love money unconditionally, not one another. So, our lives are, indeed, all about self. Our existence without unconditional love will continue, until there are no humans left, or until we humans awaken to our spiritual needs. Then, we will trust our lives to the human spirit, through sisterhood and brotherhood, once again. No more designs on the future, not even within the home. Life, in a spiritual home is governed by unspoken expectations.

But how, one might ask, would I know what is expected of me, if no one tells me? Answer: Your soul will know.

When you live in concert with what your soul knows, then your real self has a sense of place, and you feel that this world is your home. If your survival requires that you comply with directives, then, only your indoctrinated self has a sense of place, but, your feelings tell you that you are a stranger, here. You may take pleasure in the planet's beauty, but it will be as if from afar. You'll never feel part of it.

The following excerpt, taken from Bishop Curry's quote at the beginning of this chapter, bears repeating:

"Human community, human survival, human life on this planet depends on our capacity to be unselfish, to be selfless and giving. And the miracle is that when we do that, we get blessed, ourselves."

Indeed, when we are selfless and giving, in the context of sisterhood and brotherhood, Nature blesses us with unconditional love. It's through selflessness that our lives take on spiritual value—in our own eyes, and in the eyes of those who love us. In other words, the payoff for selflessness is spiritual, not material, wealth. You see, *selflessness* is *selfish*, because it's the only path to love, just as it is the only path to survival, in a world without property and money.

In his teachings, Jesus tried to convince us that selflessness is essential to our happiness. Now, "researchers all over the world" are proving it, and people like Stanly and Curry are bearing witness to it. On the day that we find ourselves trusting our lives to interdependent relationships, instead of personal wealth, we will undo what Adam and Eve did when they partook of the forbidden fruit, and our lives will again become selfless—not as a result of effort, but of what Stanly calls "Grand Design."

CHAPTER EIGHTEEN

The Serpent's False Promise

Human Evolution Stopped when Mankind Left Eden

In my view, the myth of Adam and Eve metaphorically describes a real event that originally occurred some six- to ten-thousand years ago. That event initiated a change in human life so drastic that it has inflicted on mankind an unnatural and longstanding state of suffering. The myth implies that this event was so profound as to reset the entire course of human history in an undesirable way.

Christians have long wondered what humans actually did that constituted the original sin symbolized by the eating of the apple. The authors of Genesis never said, but did provide a strong clue, by noting: *For God knows that in the day you eat thereof your eyes will be opened, and you will be like Gods, knowing good and evil*—Genesis 3:5. In other words, eating the apple symbolizes the moment in time when mankind did something that had never been done, before. Illusioned by the belief that we were capable of controlling life, we took control, through force of manmade laws, on whose authority we functioned as though we were gods.

I believe the authors of Genesis were trying to warn humanity that we had made a huge mistake by thinking we were capable of controlling life. Before that belief infected the human mind, humans had always lived within the context of Nature, as other social primates do: We lived in the moment, and reacted to changing circumstances in whatever ways we felt would best enhance our group's ability to survive.

Before people decided they could control the future, natural life was a game, in which winning meant survival. As in sports, or games of chance, the overarching atmosphere of life's game was uncertainty. But, in the natural world, no human ever faced that uncertainty, alone. Indeed, uncertainty was the key ingredient that made people passionate about life, just as we modern people are passionate about sports.

Now that we are without spiritual homes, we take no pleasure in life's uncertainties, and we're not passionate about taking care of one another. We are passionate, instead, about the need for more laws to protect ourselves from one another, and about the need to defend the institutions that impose those laws. But, laws, despite mankind's devotion to them, prevent the human spirit from performing its appointed role—the management of life's uncertainties, as they arise. This results in the accumulation of uncertainties. Trying to eliminate life's uncertainties by force of law outlaws the sensibilities of the human soul, which normally manages life's uncertainties. To do that is like crossing the event horizon of a black hole: Once crossed, there is no escaping the downward spiral of increasing uncertainty, until the effort culminates in the ultimate uncertainty—catastrophic upheaval.

In our effort to guarantee future certainty, modern humans have outlawed our emotional nature. We're no longer able to play life's game, which, before laws existed, made life's journey an interesting and challenging venture. When we were free to react to life's natural uncertainties, there was effort, spirit, enthusiasm, anticipation, the camaraderie of shared imperatives, the solidarity that primitive people experienced every moment of their lives. Little wonder that, in the midst of our "controlled" existence, we invest so much effort, time, and money in modern sports. Cut off, as we are, from life's real game, our souls seek to replicate the spirit that the game of life once universally bestowed on all humans.

In the real life of ancient humans, as in the story of Eden, the fabled "serpent" whispered an enticing idea into the human ear. It was the promise of certainty, the irresistible promise that mankind's existence would be predictable, just, and safe, if humans created a system of moral laws that authorized rights of ownership.

Humanity was so enticed by the serpent's promise that there came a day—repeated many times in various places around the world—when groups of men decided that having the right to own women would make the world a better place. To exert that right, men established systems of rules, and the punishments to enforce them.

The consequence of this act—which may well have seemed a small thing, at the time—was the institutionalization of punishments. The introduction of sanctified punishments established moral law and the concepts of good and evil, among humans. Since then, the qualities of good and evil have been ascribed to those who obey or disobey.

Unbeknownst to those men, they had just committed the "original sin" that expelled us from Eden. By compelling people to live under a system of rules, they had, in a single stroke, destroyed the natural social order among humans. And, because the human spirit evolved to live in the moment, not to follow rules, they had rendered all humans sinners—in spirit, if not in deed. Unknowingly, those men had sentenced themselves, and all the generations that followed, to the penance of a meager survival, as the abject slaves of institutions. The disorder, injustice, loneliness, poverty, and anxiety that plague modern cultures are symptoms of that bondage, which yet afflicts us.

In other words, the original sin was not the act of *defying* moral law. The original sin was to *create* it.

The idea that the world would be a better place, if men had the right to own women inspired the first moral law. But, that law looked better on paper than when put into practice. Most men don't find much satisfaction in owning women. Our problem is, once we own one, we don't know what to do with her. There she is, ready to devote her life to us. It's a devotion that most of us can't return. Indeed, wives often get mistreated as a result of their devotion, because it offends men's souls. You see, when humans lived naturally, women devoted their lives to taking care of every member of the family—their children, each other's children, their sisters, their mothers, and the brothers. Most men can't stand all that devotion to be focused on them. In the modern paradigm, we have no way to reciprocate, other than to feign devotion, by pretending we feel other than we do.

Men, too, are genetically predisposed to taking care of life, but in an entirely different way. We enjoy placing our lives on the line, for the sake of the wellbeing of the entire family, or community of families—not devoting ourselves to the needs of any individual. Having personal dependents strips men of their spiritual authority. You can't continue to take care of dependents, after dying for them. If Jesus had been married, he would never have been free to go to the cross—the act through which he exercised *his* spiritual authority.

As we have seen, the decision to grant men the right to own women hasn't worked out all that well, even for the owners. But it did establish the concept of ownership that undergirds modern civilization. Soon, men created moral laws that gave them the right to own land, animals, and slaves. But, instead of creating the certain future they intended, it separated mankind even more from life's real game— the game of life, which all animate beings love to play whether they win or lose.

The ultimate irony of humanity's "original sin," is that it really wasn't a sin, at all, despite the suffering it caused. It was a mistake that resulted from mankind's vulnerability to an idea—the infectious idea that our existence would be just and safe, if we established moral laws to regulate human behavior. We were vulnerable to making that mistake, because our emotional intelligence is incapable of warning us of that kind of danger.

Emotional intelligence is a specialized intelligence. It exists to give animate beings the kind of awareness needed for taking care of life. Each individual passes that wisdom to the successive generation, through genetic code. Thus, this wisdom has been validated and revalidated, throughout millions of years of the species' survival. One of the remarkable features of emotional intelligence is its ability to warn us of *natural* dangers, like tigers, snakes, spiders, and thousand-foot cliffs, even if we haven't previously experienced them. The fact that our emotional intelligence remains intact, even today, explains why most of us tend to fear snakes or spiders, even the ones we know are harmless.

But, emotional intelligence cannot warn us of an *unnatural* danger, like imposing moral laws, because that danger has existed for only a few thousand years. Emotional intelligence hasn't had the evolutionary time required for it to adapt, thus is unable to recognize the danger. More significantly, imposing moral laws will destroy our species in sub- evolutionary time. So, our emotional intelligence will *never* be able to warn us of the danger of instituted law. It simply doesn't have the time needed to adapt.

Unaware of the danger, the men who decided to own women did so, not because they had any evidence that the serpent's promise of certainty was true. They accepted the idea, because certainty sounded good to them, and because their emotional intelligence was unable to warn them of the trap they were setting for themselves. They were unaware that they would immediately become abject dependents of the legal systems they were creating—systems that destroyed natural social order, separating them from life's real experience, forevermore. Had they known, they never would have claimed women as property. Nor would women have tolerated being owned by men, had they understood the consequences to themselves and their children—and to life, itself.

Our blindness to the fallacy of the serpent's promise has affected far more than our personal and collective lives. It changed the course of mankind's evolution. Indeed, as a result of that error, there are now two distinct kinds of evolution: Normal evolution enables a species to flourish, over evolutionary time. Abnormal evolution enables individuals to survive the circumstances imposed by institutional law, and nothing more. When humans began living according to moral law, it ripped the foundation of human life asunder, because moral law stands in defiance of the very forces of Nature that created us. Those forces, you see, provide the field on which life's real game is played. By imposing moral laws in our belief that by honoring them we could realize a certain future, we simply abandoned the field.

As Darwin pointed out, evolution is the product of what happens when individuals, or species, perpetually compete for survival in the natural world. The best-adapted win. But, modern man suffers from the belief that institutions are sovereign, not Nature. As a result, we have fashioned countless artificial realities—human-invented fields of play—on which *our* lives play out.

On Nature's field of play, the people who are most romantically appealing are those who are genetically predisposed to take pleasure in acts of empathy, sharing, and selflessness—and in the case of males, the act of risking their lives for the sake of others. Theirs are the genes that, because they enhance a social group's ability to survive, are passed to future generations. But, on the artificial fields of play in our civilized life, ruled by money and law, the most successful—though not always—are the selfish, the schemers, the manipulators, and the greedy. In our world, it's their genes that tend to be passed on. The traits that tend to succeed, today, would not be socially acceptable in a spiritually free human culture. Consequently, individuals whose characteristics were defined by those genes would be subject to an early demise, cleansing their genes from our species' gene pool.

When I said that evolution stopped in its tracks upon mankind's exit from Eden, I did not mean that change stopped. I meant that the kinds of changes that have stopped are the ones that enable humans to flourish over evolutionary time. Evolution that serves life can only happen when a species inhabits the natural world. Unfortunately, we *moderns don't even know where the field is—where life's real game is being played*. It's a moot point, anyway, for, without our "team"—our sisters and brothers—we would not be prepared to participate, even if we knew where to join the game.

When humanity was taken in by the serpent's false promise, it was a travesty that fundamentally changed the lives of all members of our species. Since then, our spirits have no longer had any essential role to play in our lives. To this day, that status quo remains a weighty and arduous spiritual taxation on every human being. As a consequence—and so unnecessarily!—we exist without sisterhoods and brotherhoods, and without the interdependent relationships inherent to mankind's ability to survive in a world ruled by the human spirit.

In our effort to create certainty, we did the opposite. By inventing the concept of ownership, we eliminated interdependent relationships, thus depriving ourselves of the only real certainty a human being can ever experience—the certainty of knowing that, whatever difficulties the future may hold, we will give our all on behalf of our sisters and brothers, as they will for us. In life, nothing is guaranteed. But, the human spirit finds complete contentment in the certainty that our sisters and brothers will be there for us. Given that certainty, it will never ask for more, not even another day.

Remarkably, even now, the human spirit remains intact, ready to reclaim its essential role in our lives, even after thousands of years of spiritual repression imposed by mankind's belief in the law. This is evident in the selflessness experienced by those soldiers in Restrepo, and by all people, when they find themselves in circumstances of mutual dependence. The good news is that—thanks to the resilience of the human spirit—Eden yet remains accessible to humanity.

To re-enter our spiritual home, however, we need to accept life's natural uncertainties, just as all other forms of animate life do, and humans once did. In other words, stop trying to control the future by force of rules, longterm plans, and laws. To get to that point, we first need to recognize that the promise of a certain future is an illusion. *There is no such thing as a certain future*—not in the beginning, not now, not ever. That's why the mutual support of sisterhoods and brotherhoods is so essential to our sense of wellbeing.

Among people who are bonded by their need for one another, anxiety wouldn't exist. Only fear would—and only in times of *imminent* danger. And that fear would last only as long as it took for the brotherhood and sisterhood to react to the danger. As institutional dependents, however, we now live solitary lives in perpetual fear of what the future may bring, and of the "evil" people "out there," who might do harm to us, or to "our property." Indeed, that anxiety undergirds the rationale that justifies the existence of institutions and their laws.

Without the sense of wellbeing provided exclusively by sisterhoods and brotherhoods, we feel an unrelenting need for the legal systems, police forces, prisons, and armies that provide blanket protection from "all the evil, out there." Originally, institutions were created to sanctify the practice of marriage. They are now justified by our need to find relief from the anxiety we face, because we live without sisterhood or brotherhood—the very relationships the practice of marriage destroyed. Consequently, institutions are justified solely by their own existence. Had institutions never been created, sisterhood and brotherhood would still exist, and we would have no need for the "security" that institutions presume to provide.

Genetically, we haven't traveled even a few milliseconds, in evolutionary time, from where we were when we left Eden. If we modern humans were still governed by the wisdom of our souls, as were those "Edenites," we would all be like those WWII soldiers who sneaked out of field hospitals—still wounded—to rejoin their brothers on the front line. That those soldiers headed straight for danger seems strange to modern people. Of course it does! In *our* lives, there are precious few opportunities to experience the intimacy of the interdependent relationships that are so essential to emotional health. Those soldiers shared the sense of wellbeing that all humans experience, when bonded by their need for the people around them. It is a wellbeing which makes a person cognizant of life's meaning.

The universal human need for lives that feel meaningful is precisely what drove those soldiers back to be with their brothers in the most dangerous circumstances on earth. Having experienced brotherhood, before they were wounded, they were aware of where the "game of life" was being played. Their desire to rejoin the game was so profound that it seemingly didn't matter to them that the price for playing it could well be their lives. For modern people living in safe, institutionalized cocoons, there is no place at all to experience life's meaning. If there were, we too would be running for it—running to join our sisters and brothers, without concern for how it might affect our personal designs on the future.

Our spirits have no designs on the future—safe, or otherwise. Their only concern is that we be free in every moment to selflessly take care of one another, according to the wisdom of our souls. This is the only freedom that rewards us with love.

Life is dangerous. Safety is never absolute, never a given. That's why *we have spirits*—to deal with life's countless uncertainties, only one of which is danger.

Life is not about safety. It's about whether we live with love or without it. The sense of wellbeing known exclusively through love is the only connection we have to life. And life, from our spirit's perspective, is eternal. Our spirits want only the opportunity to participate in life's eternal process, regardless of what happens to *us*. On the other hand, fear of the future dissociates us from the moment, from life, and from love, thus from *everything* our souls value. That fear is the consequence of depending, for our wellbeing, on the "safe" future promised by money and law.

CHAPTER NINETEEN

Salvation Lies in Recognizing the Nature of Our Circumstances

At Woodstock we tried to let the audience know in every way we could that we believed in them. That inside them was a loving nature and a decency and fineness of spirit. You can forget it sometimes, but very few of us want to be other than that. You just need the opportunity.

From the documentary, "Woodstock—Three Days that Defined a Generation."

Perhaps you wondered, when reading the title of this chapter, why I assert that *recognition*, alone, will lead to human salvation. You may have wondered what sequence of actions would be required. If that is the case, then, you have now experienced, firsthand, how automatically modern humans assume that it takes an organized plan to solve every problem—one of the key assertions of this book.

There is a "catch 22" being revealed, here, for, to organize a plan of action *is* to remain inside the institutional paradigm. Unfortunately, this places extra locks on the cell door of our lifelong captivity to rules, laws, and plans. In natural life, the right way is about *being who we are*, not about specific or prescribed actions. Natural action occurs only upon the impetus of feelings that transmit to us the evolutionary wisdom that is ingrained in every soul.

What changes, then, when we recognize that it's our circumstances that are the problem? *We* change. Well, not really, because who we are is fixed by evolution. Though we can't change, our perspective can. Civilized people believe that if everyone did the right thing, as a result of complying with the precepts of the "right" ideology or religion, our problems would be over. We blame people for our problems, not the institutions that spiritually enslave us. That's what's got to change. We've got to recognize that spiritual enslavement is the problem, not the enslaved.

From the moment we experience that recognition, we will begin to see people in a different light. Right now, as worshippers of civil rule, we blame others for our suffering—anyone who arouses our resentment, from spouses, bosses, the president, and even ourselves. We do this, because we have been taught that, if only everyone did the right thing, obeyed the rules, then, there would be no suffering. But, once we realize that having to obey rules is the problem, we'll begin to see that there has never been anything wrong with humanity. For 6000 years, it's always been the rules! Without a viable support system, in the form of a natural human family, all of us are running scared. Real human families were destroyed by rules, long ago. People who are running scared are, indeed, not trustworthy. Without viable support systems, life is all about self. How can we really be there for each other when our lives are all about self?

Recognizing that our circumstances are the problem will start the process that reconnects us with our emotional intelligence, which evolved to guide us in our natural way of life. Our salvation requires that we trust it's guidance, which comes instinctively and unbidden, whenever we need it. To seek the guidance of anyone, any rules, any religion, or any institution would be to presume that a set of directives can replace our emotional intelligence. That is the mistake that got humanity into the painful situation we're in.

It is not the intention of this book to give anyone a new set of rules. I am telling people what I believe our circumstances are. I have come to understand that anything put into words, regarding the future, is, perforce, based on beliefs, including my own. To think of my words as gospel would be to give me the status of a god. And, frankly, I would be offended. I suffer like everyone else from institutional subjugation. I have learned much. But I am not above it all, and would appreciate being respected for that, just as I respect the reader for the suffering he or she endures. To manage my own suffering, I take great solace in the belief that our souls have the answer. We need, once again, to hear their messages, so long ignored. This book has been written to stir a reawakening among humans to the fact that we carry a treasure of wisdom in our souls. To that end, I'm posing a question to the civilized mind: How much more must we suffer, before we realize that *we have no choice but* to *surrender our designs on the future, if we are ever again to live in spiritual freedom?*

We need to understand that the future is unknowable. It cannot be controlled, longterm. Unintended consequences are always associated with any attempt to do so. The moment we take this fact to heart, a profound change will take place in our perception of what is—and is not—real: Thenceforth, we will be inoculated against illusions, never again able to take comfort in the future promised by *any* individual, institution, ideology, or religion. No such futures will any longer be real to us. That is how profoundly our perspective will change. From the depths of our souls, we will know what Jesus knew, when he was tempted on the mountain—that the promises of all the glories of the world are illusions, because they offer no spiritual rewards.

Salvation from meaninglessness is what we need. It can come only with the realization that the institutional promise of a safe and just future is an illusion. Illusions are accepted and rejected by the subconscious mind. Therefore, we can never save ourselves by conscious intent. Words, for example, can never free us from our illusions—not my words, not anyone's: No ruses, ploys, or tactics employed by the conscious mind can do that. Only the pain of spiritual repression can spark the awareness it will take to free us—*and that can happen only after we have become cognizant that institutions, not people, are the source of our suffering.*

There is a direct parallel between the emotional suffering of the 8+ billion people living on earth and the suffering experienced by Wade Robson and James Safechuk, two young men who were sexually abused by Michael Jackson, when they were boys. What's common between the suffering of both civilized people and those boys is the failure to recognize its source. Indeed, instead of recognizing it, Wade and James worshipped the source of their suffering. Their experience was dramatized in the TV special, "Oprah Winfrey Presents: After Neverland," through an in-depth discussion of the documentary, "*Leaving Neverland*," which had chronicled Michael Jackson's alleged sexual abuse of the boys.

In her commentary, Oprah said, "The reason to tell the story is because the story is bigger than any one person. Don't anyone think it's just about what Michael Jackson did or did not do. It's about this thing, this insidious pattern that's happening in our culture that we refuse to look at. I love the quote from Maureen Dowd in a column she wrote for The New York Times about celebrity superseding criminality. She said: 'How can you see clearly when you're looking into the sun? How can an icon be a con?'"

Jackson's sexual abuse of children has something in common with the emotional abuse the state imposes on us all. Both these insults to the spirit are possible, because of the brain's natural inclination to overlook the pain of the moment, in order to realize future rewards. When Oprah asked Wade why he continued his association with Jackson, after having been abused, he replied: "I had no sense of it being abuse. I loved Michael. When I testified on his behalf and gushed over him publicly, that was from a real place."

Despite what Michael was accused of doing, he was a remarkable person in most ways, and made a real difference in the lives of many children, through philanthropy. Most importantly, though, he had celebrity. Without them realizing it, the boys' association with Michael placed them in a world that was so grand and magical that the discomfort of being sexually abused was subconsciously repressed to the point of nonexistence.

Celebrity has power, but the power of the institutions that dominate all humanity far exceeds it. An institution's standing in society supersedes that of any individual. By enabling humans to organize en masse, institutions make possible a world of conveniences that otherwise could not exist. More significantly, they give us the right to live on land within their jurisdiction, through citizenship. So, we love our institutions for the same reason those boys loved Michael, because of the possibilities they offer.

As a result of our love for institutions, human minds have gone thousands of years without ever associating the pain of spiritual repression with its source—institutional subjugation. Therefore, we have lived for countless generations with a pain we inflicted on ourselves, by allowing legal systems to repress the feelings that arise from our souls. We act as if the pain doesn't exist. When civilized people "gush" over their institutions, as when they pledge allegiance to their governments, salute their flags, and kill or die on their government's behalf, that, too, comes "from a real place."

In Wade's mind, the pain of having been sexually abused by Jackson was so dissociated from its source that it wasn't until his second nervous breakdown, as an adult, that he began to suspect that his problems had something to do with what had happened to him as a child. His first step toward recovery was the hardest—to admit to himself and his family that he had been sexually abused.

Humanity, too, is suffering, but in our case it's from the spiritual abuse of our submission to institutionally imposed law. Recognition—the first step in our recovery—will also be the hardest, because we, too, will have to admit to ourselves that we are being emotionally abused by the institutions we worship. That conscious recognition will place people who experience it in a state of shock, just as it did me, years ago.

Recovering from that shock will emotionally release us from our institutional cages. For the first time in our lives, we will be in touch with, and informed by, the wisdom of human nature that grounds us in the reality that sustains the life of our species. A victory of the spirit. A victory for life.

In that moment of victory, we will be emotionally transported outside our cages, and into the real world, where there are no beliefs, dreams, or idealized futures in which to take comfort. Physically, though, we will still be inside our institutional cages. We'll still need property and a personal store of wealth to survive. And we will remain subjects of the state. In other words, we'll still have to behave as if we *are* in control of our futures. The difference is, we'll no longer believe in anything we are doing—neither in the future we once strived for, nor in the sovereignty of any state.

How will we manage the pain of going through the motions of modern life, when we no longer believe in what we are doing? We won't manage it—not at first, anyhow. I know, because I've been there.

Years ago, my sense of purpose was largely based on the belief that I was making the world a better place, by developing missile guidance systems, to defend the institutions I worshipped. Then, I realized that institutions are falsely justified by the belief that we can make the future knowable, by force of law. As a result of my knowledge about system control theory I realized that the future cannot, in fact, be controlled. Suddenly I saw my work as facilitating the mass killing of humans to defend institutions that ultimately can't be defended. Instead of making the world a better place, I was participating in a futile cause.

That's how I ended up emotionally outside the institutional cage. More problematic, still, was my realization that, as a subject of the state, I had devoted my entire life to trying to control my own destiny. To me, this rendered meaningless everything I had ever done.

This realization put me in a state of shock so severe that I couldn't see the ground—not because it wasn't there, but because, emotionally, my life suddenly had nothing to stand on. Having been emotionally cast out of the institutional cage, I found myself bereft of any belief system to provide comfort. There followed an extended period, during which I thought that, for the rest of my life, I would never again experience any kind of good feeling. At times, I cried out loud, to the heavens: "Why did this have to happen to me?"

But it is one of the graces of Nature that the mind can recover from any shock. As a result, though I remain emotionally outside the cage, I am now finding my life rather agreeable, out here. It's far more agreeable than it was when I was still justifying my activities in the belief that I could control my own destiny, and that controlling it would have meaning, beyond mere survival.

Though I live alone, I take comfort in the relationships I have with my family—which included my ex-wife, Joyce, when she was still alive. I also enjoy meaningful relationships with the motorcyclists with whom I ride. However, I avoid personal relationships with women. It's not that I don't like them, or that I don't miss the tenderness and ecstasy of a romantic embrace, as much as anyone. It's just that I've learned that women, by their very nature, have expectations in relationships that, given the circumstances of modern life, I cannot fulfill—not even by pretending. This ultimately results in women becoming disappointed with me, something that pains me, perhaps as much as it does them. I feel quite certain that I wasn't put on earth to disappoint women. So, until women start forming sisterhoods, through which their inborn expectations regarding relationships *can* be fulfilled, it's best that I just stay away.

I will say this, about my experience of having been emotionally cast out of the institutional cage. No one who sees through an illusion will ever regret it, regardless of the pain—particularly the illusion that humans need institutions to protect them from one another in order to live on earth. It is a blessing to realize that it is not people, but institutional subjugation, that is the cause of our unnatural state of suffering. When we understand that, we will see that people are born with the innate need to celebrate life through their relationships—a need that largely goes unsatisfied in our present, spiritually alienated, way of life. I am writing this book in the hope that, someday, people will regain their spiritual freedom, so they can return to the natural human way of life.

My recovery from my own state of shock was particularly diffi-cult, because I was alone, in my shock. No one else had any idea why

I was in such a distraught state of mind. Fortunately, I made enough sense in explaining myself, that no one suggested I should be put into the looney bin (as far as I know). Still, no one really got the picture. When it finally became evident that I was going to recover, I took some pride in the fact that I had been able to survive it, at all.

As-yet unanswered is the question of when more individuals will find themselves outside the institutional cage. The inherent instability of mass cultures causes the pain of institutional subjugation to keep intensifying, until the institutions that govern the cultures fail. As that pain intensifies in our world, more and more individuals may well find themselves outside the institutional cage, and come to see the world as I have described it in this book. Once out of the cage, they will recognize that all beliefs are illusions. Their instincts will come to the fore, and will provide them all with one world view. Left behind will be the countless conflicting world views that belief-based realities impose. The shock, itself, will be the impetus, and one shared world view will be the means, to draw them together, in sisterhoods and brotherhoods— the only viable support system for human beings, and the only home in which humans can celebrate life.

Regardless of how lost, or even stunned, we feel, we will eventually recover from the shock of recognizing that the future is uncontrollable, as surely as our predecessors recovered from the shock of realizing that we don't live at the center of the universe.

It is precisely because the future is uncontrollable that natural life is a journey in which to participate, not a goal to be achieved. Once we are cognizant of that, we will begin to see through the countless beliefs that now blind us to the evolutionary wisdom of our souls. These illusions will begin to dissolve, one by one, slowly at first, then faster, until the reality of life one-day snaps into focus. It will be the reality perceived through our innate wisdom, a reality without beliefs, property rights, longterm plans, dreams, or sovereign states. Though that reality will lack many things we now believe are essential, in it we will find something precious that we lost, 6000 years ago. We will rediscover the wisdom of human nature, without whose guidance real contentment is impossible.

Though it will be radically new to us, this is the ageless reality in which all animate beings evolved to live. It's the reality where success, happiness, contentment, commitment, engagement, and fulfillment result exclusively from being who we are, not who we're supposed to be. When we recognize this as the reality for which Nature designed us, we will be fully cognizant of the wisdom of our souls, and will welcome the relationships of sisterhood and brotherhood.

I would love to tell you what the intimacy of sisterhood and brotherhood feels like. Unfortunately, I can't, even though—on two separate occasions—I have experienced sisterly-brotherly love in the same sense that those young people did at Woodstock. Trying to explain what that intimacy feels like would be like trying to explain romantic love to someone who has never experienced its feelings. The unconditional love of sisterhood and brotherhood is exactly like the intimacy of romance, at least in one way: Circumstances bring it about, not intent. Sisterly and brotherly love occur only in circumstances in which people are taking care of life, in their service to the people around them.

As we merge with others who have been emotionally released from their cages, the answers to the question of what to do will be as self-evident to us as knowing to eat, when hungry. Seamlessly, we will fall into the natural human way of life in which we do what Nature created us to do—fully enjoying the process of attending to one another's present needs and letting the future take care of itself. In the atmosphere of intimacy and mutual support that springs from selflessness and from caring, spiritual homes will naturally form, bringing the contentment of sisterhood and brotherhood into our lives. Then, for the first time in our lives, we will know why we are here.

As for the question of *how* we will take care of one another, let's follow Jesus's advice, and not worry about it. To address that matter before sisterhoods and brotherhoods can even reassert themselves is to put the cart before the horse. The wisdom of human nature evolved to answer that question for us, but its answers apply only in the unfolding moment—never to the unknowable future. Presuming to have the answers about how we are going to take care of each other in the distant future prevents our innate wisdom from ever having an opportunity to address the matter. This is the crux of the modern human dilemma: As long as we continue to put the cart before the horse, our souls' wisdom will not only remain excluded from our lives, its repression at the hands of rules and plans will be the principal source of our suffering.

CHAPTER TWENTY

The Chain Reaction that Will Change Everything

Despite the astonishing things that humans are capable of doing, we remain unsure of our goals and we seem to be as discontented as ever. We have advanced from canoes to galleys to steamships to space shuttles—but nobody knows where we're going. We are more powerful than ever before, but have very little idea what to do with all that power. Worse still, humans seem to be more irresponsible than ever. Self-made gods with only the laws of physics to keep us company, we are accountable to no one. We are consequently wreaking havoc on our fellow animals and on the surrounding ecosystem, seeking little more than our own comfort and amusement, yet never finding satisfaction. Is there anything more dangerous than dissatisfied and irresponsible gods who don't know what they want?

–final words in the book, "Sapiens," by Yuval Noah Harari

If you read Genesis, you'll know that its authors believed humans would never regain their spiritual freedom. Their metaphorical description of the angel with a flaming sword—placed there by God to guard the path to the tree of life—makes that clear. (Genesis 3:24)

As we modern people confront the question of how to undo humanity's six-thousand-year-old blunder, we run the risk of erring again, by taking it on as *a task—a responsibility*. But that would do nothing but prolong our bondage. So, it's important that we gird ourselves with the conscious conviction that *social change made by intent always results in spiritual repression.* We know that our spirits evolved to celebrate *what is.* We also know that, in natural life, there is no "supposed-to-be." That knowledge is really all we need to set in motion the freeing of humanity.

Given the difficulty involved in freeing ourselves from the grip of institutional subjugation, you may find it counterintuitive of me, to boldly state that there is nothing to stop us from regaining our spiritual freedom. But it's true—true, because our most priceless asset is the indestructibility of our human spirits, which six thousand years of repression have failed to silence, and will never silence, as long as humans walk upon the earth.

Clearly, our spirits are still intact, still communicating our souls' messages. Otherwise, we wouldn't suffer! What's hard is that we can't *make* the change happen. It can't be engineered. It must be *allowed* to happen. This inner transition—delicate, but worldchanging—this release of the spirit, calls on us to stay focused on the key necessity, which is a matter of *relearning* our native trust in our Nature-given emotional intelligence. A part of relearning is remembering that this intelligence was born into us, so that we can take care of life—not control it! Our 6000-year attempt to control behavior, to bring about a certain future, profoundly offends the wisdom of our souls, and is the source of modern man's unnatural state of suffering.

The opposite of making life happen according to plan is *letting it happen*. We have to *let life find its own way,* in the same sense that a stream of water finds its own way. This is the way that our real selves will be righted, our natural human way of life renewed, our spiritual connections rejoined, our relationships reconstituted, and our sense of wellbeing and belonging re-ignited in the human breast. All this! And no need for us to *do* anything, other than honor our real selves, the selves Nature created.

It's not easy, of course, for indoctrinated people to renounce life-long beliefs—to learn to feel, again, the touch of the soul's wisdom that our ancestors abandoned, so long ago. Of course it's not easy. We are steeped in the illusion that human beings are in control. Every detail of our lives is defined by that illusion. Personally and collectively, we see ourselves as responsible—for everything, including our own suffering. Because of the illusion that we're in control, we seek relief by applying more control, or by changing ourselves. Both of these are recipes for disaster that only bury us deeper in our problems. You see, *control is the problem*. We, the beings Nature created, are not.

Our role in healing the human condition is to pull up the roots of our illusion of control through the simple act of *recognizing, and accepting* our true nature as human beings. Recognition is the match that lights the spark. Then, like everything natural, the answer will unfold as it unfolds—not by our intent, not at our command. It falls to us to know and accept that it may never happen—and to understand that, if it does happen, the solution will come in a way that's least expected.

What we do not need, for certain, is more control, such as more laws, more enforcement, more surveillance, or a world government. What we need—each of us—is to find what the spiritual repression so rampant in civilized life has kept hidden from mankind for thousands of years. We need to discover what I think Jesus discovered—and what I believe all humans felt prior to the existence of culturally imposed moral edicts:

There exists within every human being a real self, which values the existence of life more than it values its own existence. It desires only the opportunity to participate in life's eternal process. This is the self that is free of the need to control, because it is invested in the wellbeing of *life* far more than in the wellbeing of *self*.

Spiritual freedom, when it comes, will be experienced in the form of sisterly-brotherly love. As with romantic love and motherly love, no one can make sisterly-brotherly love happen. *We do not control love.* Love happens spontaneously when the circumstances are right, as judged by the wisdom of our souls. Sisterly-brotherly love happens spontaneously among people whose souls are free to place life's needs above their own in relationships of mutual dependence.

Sisterly-brotherly love cannot happen under the duress created by plans and rules. Longterm commitments cause our minds to focus on the future, which forces us into a state of spiritual dishonesty—the antithesis of love. Rules are *based* on spiritual distrust—the belief that, my sisters and brothers are *not there for me*, thus, I need protection *from* them. Plans and rules force everyone to put their own imagined future needs above life's real and present needs. This destroys sisterly-brotherly love. It destroys spiritual freedom. It destroys life. And, if allowed to continue, it will eventually denature the planet.

For reasons that I trust are now obvious to the reader, I can offer no specific plan or procedure for making sisterly-brotherly love happen. I have explained the nature of our circumstances, as I see them, as clearly as I can. I've described, in particular, the simple mistake mankind made that cast us out from our natural way of life, by depriving us of our spiritual freedom. With that knowledge in mind, and despite the spiritual repression inherent to our present way of life, I hold great hope that we, the people, will find reason to let our spirits out of the closet of distrust and shame, so they can again show us the way.

I believe that enough people will come to recognize the need to surrender their designs on the future. I don't know when or how that will happen. But, I have no doubt that, once it does, their spirits will find each other. Spontaneously, in their souls' recognition of their need for one another, sisterly-brotherly love will happen. One after another, natural families will form, as in a chain reaction—a phenomenon that may well become contagious, given the dramatic difference in the feeling of natural freedom from the social bondage we now endure. This will be a chain reaction that changes everything, a chain reaction on which, in my view, the future of humanity rests.

What will the world look like, when mankind regains spiritual freedom? That is not for us to know. In any case, having the answer would change nothing. Our only viable concern is attaining the freedom to be true to our real selves, in our relationships with the people around us. When we are real, our spirits repose in the abiding, soul-felt sense that life is in good hands. When we are real, only the present matters. The future—even our own—will be of no concern to us.

CODA

The Coronavirus Crisis—
A Lesson on Spiritual Connection

The situation is very scary and very real, but the camaraderie at work is something I've never seen before. It's usually like, you can't wait to get off work, because it's been a busy day, and you just want to go home. But now, when you're home, you just want to be at work.

—Elyse Isopo, critical care nurse at North Shore University Hospital, Long Island NY, during the Coronavirus crisis.

During the coronavirus pandemic, retired doctors and nurses are volunteering by the thousands, at risk to their own lives, to serve those in need. CEO's are taking huge pay cuts—or no remunerations at all—to ease the burdens on their employees. Celebrities are donating millions. Legislative bodies are attending to real and present needs, rather than remaining ideologically incapacitated.

These people are behaving "unnaturally" in a remarkable way! I say "unnaturally," because we civilized people normally spend our lives focused on realizing personal ambitions. During times of crisis, however, people are naturally inspired to serve others, even at the risk of their own wellbeing. Are these people crazy, or is "normal" civilized behavior what's crazy? These two kinds of behavior could not differ more. One is focused almost entirely on serving self, the other on serving others. They can't both be normal.

What is normal human behavior? Civilized people think our present way of life is natural. It's difficult for us to appreciate the fact that our six thousand years of human civilization represent only milliseconds in evolutionary time. Before civil rule, there were no mass cultures, thus, no rules, laws or moral values to live by. People survived by taking care of one another in the context of intimate, interdependent relationships. But, we moderns are subjects of civil rule, so we depend on money for survival, not each other. This artificial dependence has broken the spiritual connections inherent to humankind's natural way of life.

Yet, emotionally, we remain the same beings that humans were long before mass cultures existed. So, when facing a crisis, our emotions impel us to respond just as our distant ancestors did, who lived in intimate cultures. Crisis situations remind us of something that our predecessors could never have forgotten: *We are all in this together*. Instantly, this sense of togetherness restores our spiritual connections, and we find ourselves placing the needs of others above our own. We don't realize it, but these spiritual connections are the same ones that once bonded natural human families in a state of unconditional love. With our concerns for one another restored, our common sensibilities reassert themselves, and we moderns understand what all humans knew, when we depended on each other to survive—that serving the needs of others, not our own, is what's important, if we want to participate in life.

It is my assertion that, because we are hard-wired for interdependent relationships, no human is whole without them. Bestselling author Brené Brown, who writes about the connection between vulnerability and love, apparently agrees. When asked, on CBS's 60 Minutes, if her books are found in the "self-help" section, she replied, "Yes, but that bugs the hell out of me. I don't think we're supposed to help ourselves. We're supposed to help each other. My message is clear. We are neuro-biologically hardwired to be in connection with other people." A notable quote by late author Joseph Campbell seems to reveal that he, too, recognized the seriousness of our emotional predicament: He said, *I don't believe people are looking for the meaning of life as much as they are looking for the experience of being alive.*

No lesson is worth the terrible price the Coronavirus is exacting, in human suffering. But, living through it has already given many an unanticipated glimpse of what it means to be human. As people like Elise Isopo, quoted above, and countless others, respond to this crisis, their lives are being stamped with unforgettable memories, through temporarily sharing the profound experience *of being alive.*

Comparing Realities		
Natural Human Needs	Spiritually Based Reality	Legally Imposed Reality
Relationships	**Based on Feelings** People serve life through interdependent relationships. They are rewarded, for being true to life, with unconditional love for one another. The resulting bonds become increasingly unbreakable, with every challenge they face. Relationships that do not serve life disband under the duress of spiritual alienation.	**Based on Legal Commitments** People pairbond to satisfy moral edicts. This precludes the love through which evolution rewards all beings for serving life. Typically, couples experience pain—mild, for some, for others unbearable—which they endure, if they can, or put to an end, by disbanding (divorcing) or living separately.
Success and Security	**Social Acceptance** The key to an individual's survival is social acceptance by the members of an extended family. Being shunned is the ultimate failure—a failure that will likely cost the individual his life, since homo sapiens are neither physically nor emotionally equipped to survive the natural world, without the support of an extended family.	**Wealth and Privilege** Success is one-dimensional. Personal wealth is the only source of security that institutionally subjugated people have. Without economic success—a category of achievement that doesn't exist in Nature—people suffer spiritual insult as wards of the state, or suffer the material and spiritual insult, of homelessness.
A Place to Live	**Territory** People secure a place to live through territorial claims made by the family, or larger community of families. To validate a territorial claim in the eyes of the human spirit, the people who make the claim must occupy the territory and be prepared to defend it, as the land on whose resources they depend for survival.	**Property** People secure a place to live through ownership. An individual doesn't need to occupy property, to own it, nor is there a limit to how much he can own, making ownership unrelated to human need. Indeed, by granting the owner godlike status over what he owns, the state becomes the owner's god, which is why civilized people kill and die on behalf of states, in the universal belief that God is on their side.

Natural Human Needs	Spiritually Based Reality	Legally Imposed Reality
Order	**Is Natural** Because survival is dependent on social acceptance, disorder offers no benefit to the disorderly. Disorder is therefore exclusively caused by brains that are dysfunctional, to which the family must react, particularly if the individual is dangerous. But in doing whatever must be done, they recognize that the individual is behaviorally disfigured, not evil, or at fault.	**Imposed by Law** Order is civilization's Achilles Heel. Laws codify human behavior by prescribing what's good and what's evil. They require jurisdictions to occupy, police to enforce, prisons to punish, and machines of war to protect. There is no evidence that "the law" can make good on its promise of eternal order. By trusting the law, we are imprisoning our spirits and ignoring the lessons of history.
Meaning, Fulfillment, & Contentment	**Implicit** Guided by evolutionary wisdom, all beings naturally serve their purpose—to ensure that the cycle of life continues. For this, their souls reward them with an abiding sense of meaning, fulfillment and contentment. <u>People live in the moment</u>. They learn from experience, not words, books, or beliefs. With innate feelings to guide them, they are true to themselves, and to life.	**Found in the Promises of Beliefs** People are not free to serve life. Thus, they are reduced to finding whatever contentment is possible through the promise of wealth, beliefs, and dreams. <u>People live for the future</u>. We think that by behaving according to the dictates of the law, we can realize the objectives for which we dream—even though we have no proof that realizing our objectives would result in the contentment we seek.
Education	**Apprenticeship** Children learn from experience. They gravitate to activities in which they have inherent interest. Taught by skilled individuals, they emerge ready to use their expertise to serve their community, as adults.	**Formal** To attain the knowledge needed for economic success requires one to endure the spiritual insult of years of formal education in subjects for which the individual often has little or no inherent interest.
Sex	**Controlled by innate wisdom** Sexual intercourse satisfies romantic feelings that express our species' sensibilities about procreation and genetic selection. When romance is satisfied, the relationship returns to what it was before.	**Controlled by moral edicts** Cultural mores prohibit sexual intercourse outside of marriage. The father—a relationship unknown among other social primates—is thus morally obligated to share in caring for his progeny.

Natural Human Needs	Spiritually Based Reality	Legally Imposed Reality
Medium of Exchange	**None** Spiritually free people are sustained by the land from which they secure nourishment, clothing, and shelter. They occasionally barter. But the value is in the things exchanged. They use no universally accepted medium of exchange, which would require the police powers of a state to authorize, and a vault or temple to protect.	**Money** Use of money renders irrelevant the interdependent relationships through which humans naturally attain their material needs— the very relationships that are mankind's only access to sisterly and brotherly love. Trying to fill, with material things, the void of not being loved makes us materialistic. Money, not life, owns our souls. We know that to uncover the crimes we commit against one another, just follow the money. Likewise, to uncover the "crimes" we commit against our own souls, life, and the environment, just follow the money. In short, money is not compatible with human happiness, or with human existence.
Family Size	**Limited by Inherent Social Structures** In all social species, family size is determined by the genetic code that evolved to enable the species to flourish. The "survival unit" for social species is the extended family. Its optimal size varies by species, and does not significantly change from location to location.	**Unlimited** A pairbond, which we think of as family, exists to satisfy moral edicts. A pairbond is not a survival unit. Institutionalizing family relationships destroys human survival units. By default, states have become our survival units. Instead of depending on the members of our extended family to survive, we depend on the state to protect us from one another. But, in that dependency, we pay a terrible emotional price, in the form of anxiety, loneliness, and family dysfunction. Deprived of the freedom to serve our purpose through interdependent human relationships, we live lives of quiet desperation.
Beliefs	**In What Feels Good** Every feeling can be satisfied by doing something, or the feeling wouldn't exist. To serve life, spiritually free people do what feels good, and avoid activities that cause pain.	**In the promise of beliefs** Satisfaction that results from acting on innate feelings is prohibited. People make do with beliefs that promise future satisfaction—the promises of law, money, religion, institutions, nationalism, ideology, science, progress, karma, reincarnation, etc.

Glossary of Terms

Beliefs—Promises about the future, which humans accept as truths, but which are irrational, because they cannot be verified, until the future actually arrives.

Civilizational failure-The end of a civilization, which occurs when the system of laws on which a civilization is founded results in so much suffering that people revolt against the system, or will no longer defend it against invading forces.

Civilized paradigm—The framework of presumptions defining modern life, in which life is governed by manmade laws justified by the belief that the future must be controlled.

Culturally imposed dementia—Dysfunctional behavior caused by civilized human's belief that the unknowable future can be made knowable by force of manmade laws.

Earthly Eden—Not a place, but the context in which people lived, prior to the existence of culturally imposed rules and laws.

Emotional bondage—See spiritual imprisonment.

Emotional freedom—See Spiritual Freedom.

Emotional intelligence—The instinctive feelings that all animate beings experience, which inspire each individual to react to every situation in a way that serves life; The evolutionary wisdom stored in our genetic code.

Emotional alienation—See social isolation.

Evolutionary birthright—The inborn right of every animate being to live in spiritual freedom, according to the sensibilities written into its genetic code.

Evolutionary paradigm—The natural order in which life unfolds according to instincts honed by evolution, over millions of years.

Evolutionary role—The specific roles that evolution assigns to males and females, through which each sex serves the life of the species.

Feelings of the moment—Feelings, such as anger, romance, hunger, empathy, thirst, etc., that arise from instinct, in response to immediate circumstances.

Illusioned mind—A mind that accepts the promises of beliefs as true; See also: Beliefs; Religious beliefs; Secular beliefs.

Institutional bondage—See Spiritual imprisonment.

Institutional paradigm—See Civilizational paradigm

Institutionally imposed laws—Laws imposed by governments to enforce uniformity of behavior throughout a mass culture, for the purpose of controlling the future.

Interdependent relationships—Relationships characterized by the intimacy of brotherly and sisterly love, in which people depend on each other to survive; See also: Circumstances of unconditional love; Unconditional love; Spiritual home; Survival unit.

Languaged brain—The unique human attribute responsible for the invention of civilization, its institutions, and laws. It gave humans the ability to imagine the future, discuss it, fear it, and desire to control it.

Legal and monetary identity—The paper identity that defines the rights, privileges, and status of every individual in a civil culture.

Legally bonded—Bonded by legal commitments.

Living in the moment—Living, not by plans and aspirations, but according to how one feels in response to the everchanging nuances of the present moment.

Map of life—Instincts which inform all animate beings about how to react to any situation encountered in Nature. Think of our instincts as Nature's GPS, except the output is expressed through feelings, not arrows on a map, and the object is to perpetuate the cycle of life, instead of arriving at a distant location.

Moral edicts—Legally imposed moral principles.

Moral truths—Culturally agreed-upon definitions of what is good or evil, to justify laws through which humans attempt to control the future.

Motherly love—The unconditional love through which a mother's innate wisdom rewards her for nurturing her young.

Mythology of Eden—The mythological story, from the Book of Genesis, which tells how humans fell from grace, by committing the original sin; See also: Original error.

Natural emotions—The feelings that arise from our instincts, which governed life, prior to the existence of civil rule.

Natural extended family—A family bonded by the interdependent relationships required to survive the natural world; See also: Natural human family; Spiritual home; Survival unit.

Natural social order—An order that is established and maintained exclusively by the emotional intelligence of the participants; The order that existed among humans, prior to mass cultures—and still exists, today, among all other social species.

Offense to life—Behavior whose eventual effect is to diminish the species' ability to survive.

Original error—The mistake humanity made by inventing civilization, which institutionalized human relationships under moral law; See also: Mythology of Eden.

Original sin—The error humanity committed by creating moral law. See also: Original error.

Pre-humans—The social primates from which homo sapiens evolved.

Religious beliefs—Beliefs in supernatural forces and beings that bring meaning to the lives of people who are not free to experience life's natural meaning, by living in the moment.

Romantic love—The unconditional love through which evolution rewards couples for procreating.

Secular beliefs—Beliefs in the promises of money, ideologies, education, technology and science that bring meaning to the lives of people who are not free to experience life's natural meaning, by living in the moment.

Sensibilities of the soul—The evolutionary wisdom contained in the soul, which inspires the behavior needed for the species to flourish; Common sense.

Serving life—Behaving in ways that optimize the likelihood that the species will flourish.

Sisterhoods—The socially and spiritually bonded women who form the core of natural human families.

Sisterly and Brotherly love—The unconditional love people experience in groups, when depending on each other, to survive; See also: Unconditional love.

Social acceptability—The key to survival in a natural human culture, without which an individual can't participate in the life of an extended family.

Social intelligence—See emotional intelligence.

Social isolation—The emotional suffering social beings experience, when living without the intimacy inherent to interdependent relationships.

Social primates—Primates who live in closely related interdependent groups.

Spiritual authority of sisterhoods—The unique power of female sensibilities, to prevail when females are naturally bonded in spiritual freedom; The natural authority that validates sisterhoods as the core of natural human families.

Spiritual dishonesty—Pretending to feel other than we really do, in order to fit in and maintain our station in a civil culture; The betrayal of our own spirit, the spirits of those around us, and of life-itself, by repressing our true feelings, in order to comply with the impositions of civil rule.

Spiritual distrust—The belief that humans are inherently untrustworthy, thus need legal systems to protect them from one another.

Spiritual trust—The belief—intrinsic to spiritually free humans—that our brothers and sisters will give their all for us, as we will for them, come hell or high water; The belief—lacking in modern humans—that all beings, human and animal, possess the emotional intelligence needed to serve life.

Spiritual freedom—The freedom to behave in ways that satisfy the instinctive emotions that arise from the soul, in light of the situation at hand; The state of being free of rules, plans, and prescribed commitments; The freedom to answer to our souls; The freedom to be true to ourselves.

Spiritual home—A family whose members are spiritually bonded, thus, spiritually free. See also: Extended family; survival unit.

Spiritual imprisonment—The emotional state of human beings who are subject to rules, laws, longterm plans, and prescribed commitments.

Spiritual wealth—The contentment, commitment, and sense of freedom experienced by humans living in the state of unconditional love.

Spiritually bonded—Bonded by feelings of romantic love, motherly love, or brotherly and sisterly love. See also: Unconditional love

Survival unit—The optimal number of members, of a given species, needed to form a group large enough to survive the natural world.

Unconditional love—The love with which our souls reward us for serving life, through mutual cooperation; See also: Romantic love; Motherly love; Sisterly and Brotherly love.

Unillusioned mind—A mind that learns exclusively from experience, lives in the moment, and holds no beliefs that promise a better future; A spiritually free mind.

Unnatural emotions—The feelings that salve the emotional pain modern humans suffer from institutional subjugation, when they accept the unverifiable promises of beliefs in better futures.

Viable family relationships—Relationships through which humans serve life, in their service to one another; The foundational element in the survival of any social species.

Q: What makes people happy?

A: Doing what we feel like doing:

Eating when hungry
Expressing anger when we feel anger
Attending to the needs of people we love
Finding others to be with, when lonely

We don't need a formal education to be happy.
We're born with everything we need to know.

196

Evolution is as much about Happiness as it is about Species Survival

Order in Nature
Results when animals do what they feel like doing. It's not a perfect order, or a perfect happiness, but is sufficient for life to flourish on this planet

Order in Civilization
Results from people complying with rules, laws, and legal arrangements. People are rarely free to do what they feel like doing, and we're not very happy. Civil order is destroying life on this planet.

The Foundation for Order and Survival is Family

Natural order is about species survival

- Social primates need each other to survive. By bonding in extended families, they fulfill spiritual obligations that serve life. Their need for one another maintains the natural order required for the species to flourish.

Civil order is about survival of the state

- Modern humans need money to survive. We pairbond to fulfill legal obligations that maintain the order required for the state to survive.

Love is not something we do.
It's something we need.

We don't love people because they need us.

- *We love them because we need them—the greater our need, the greater our love.*
- *If we need them to survive, our love for them is unconditional.*
- *Social primates in the wild love unconditionally, because they need each other to survive.*

Civilized people love money unconditionally.

- *We need money to survive.*
- *We exist largely without unconditional love.*

Sisterhood is the core of social primate families

Humans are social primates:

- Evolution commissioned females to take care of life.

- Evolution commissioned males to protect life.

- It takes far more emotional intelligence to take care of life, than to protect it. That's why, in women's eyes, men never grow up.

- Since mankind began the practice of pairbonding, the social status of women has been subordinate to that of men. _If life is ever again to be taken care of, that's got to change._

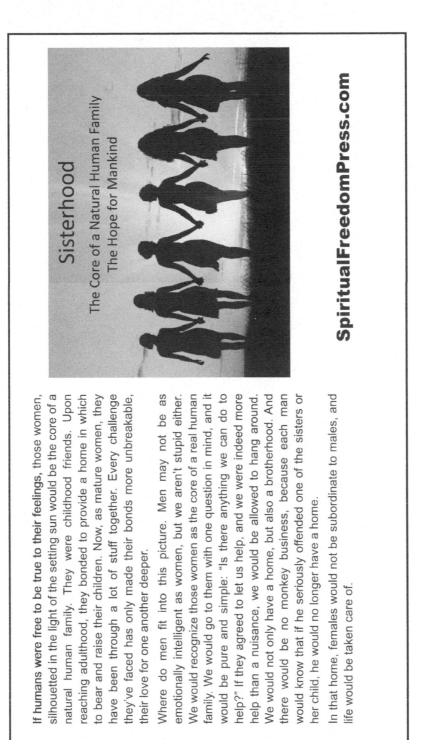

Sisterhood

The Core of a Natural Human Family

The Hope for Mankind

SpiritualFreedomPress.com

If humans were free to be true to their feelings, those women, silhouetted in the light of the setting sun would be the core of a natural human family. They were childhood friends. Upon reaching adulthood, they bonded to provide a home in which to bear and raise their children. Now, as mature women, they have been through a lot of stuff together. Every challenge they've faced has only made their bonds more unbreakable, their love for one another deeper.

Where do men fit into this picture. Men may not be as emotionally intelligent as women, but we aren't stupid either. We would recognize those women as the core of a real human family. We would go to them with one question in mind, and it would be pure and simple: "Is there anything we can do to help?" If they agreed to let us help, and we were indeed more help than a nuisance, we would be allowed to hang around. We would not only have a home, but also a brotherhood. And there would be no monkey business, because each man would know that if he seriously offended one of the sisters or her child, he would no longer have a home.

In that home, females would not be subordinate to males, and life would be taken care of.

"In small, intimate groups, feelings once were the guides for our decisions and actions, because life unfolded right in front of us, inside of each moment. Nothing more needed to be known. Call it direct living, and call ours indirect. Then, think of all the myriad ways our lives have become indirect, with abstract problems to solve, using secondhand information. Think of that, and you will grasp the drastic difference between our complicated, indexed and enumerated, terribly oblique world and the straightforward, life-essential world that cradled humanity." —Marianne Ferrari

During my stay with the Yanomami, I have realized that we have so much to learn and gain from such a great and proud people. Though their village has no written language, no calendar, does not count beyond two and is unaware of what is beyond their tropical borders, I have learned and experienced the essence of what it is to be human. The Yanomami, free from distractions and woes of modern technology and societal strife, are intimately intertwined with the environment and have taught me genuine human interaction. —David Good, "The Good Project"

Life is dangerous. Safety is never absolute, never a given. That's why we have spirits—to deal with life's countless uncertainties, only one of which is danger. Life is not about safety. It's about whether we live with love or without it. The sense of wellbeing known exclusively through love is the only connection we have to life. And life, from our spirit's perspective, is eternal. Our spirits want only the opportunity to participate in life's eternal process, regardless of what happens to us. On the other hand, fear of the future dissociates us from the moment, from life, and from love, thus from everything our souls value. That fear is the consequence of depending, for our wellbeing, on the "safe" future promised by money and law.
—Chet Shupe

About the Author

Chet Shupe is an electronics engineer who once suffered profound Attention Deficit Disorder (A D D). With A D D, social relationships baffled him. After years of bewilderment and depression, his condition was finally diagnosed, and effectively treated by the drug Ritalin. Suddenly, at 43, life made sense.

Shupe emerged from A D D with a unique perspective on the human condition. His engineer's mind forced him to ask basic questions about the brain's purpose, how the mind is organized, why feelings exist, the origin of good and evil, the true dynamics of every relationship, and how all of this relates to our happiness and to the wellbeing of humanity.

For years, Shupe has pursued his inquiry with passion and conviction, ranging far into the intricacies of the modern social contract, to question how well it is serving us, both individually and collectively. As a scientist, he bolsters every conclusion with logical and compelling examples. As a person of feeling and intuition, he expresses his hopes for humanity with genuine compassion and sincerity. As a whistleblower to the world, he speaks with urgency about the need to rediscover our connections with our own Nature, if we are ever again to experience the contentment of sisterhood and brotherhood that is our natural heritage.

We come into the world needing others.
Then we are told it's braver to go it alone.
That independence is the way to accomplish.

But there's another way to live.
A way that sees the only path to fulfillment – is through others.
That our time here can be deep beyond measure.

No one who chose interdependence ever found despair.
Because what the world taught as weakness,
is in fact our greatest virtue. —Author unknown

SpiritualFreedomPress.com